I0062370

F-U
MONEY

F-U MONEY

WHAT THE RICH DON'T HAVE THE BALLS TO TELL YOU

TAY SWEAT

SECURE THE BAG
EDUCATION

COPYRIGHT © 2023 TAY SWEAT

All rights reserved.

F-U MONEY

What the Rich Don't Have the Balls to Tell You

ISBN 978-1-5445-3191-5 *Hardcover*

   978-1-5445-3190-8 *Paperback*

   978-1-5445-3189-2 *Ebook*

CONTENTS

Whatever you say you are or aren't, whatever you say you can or can't do...you're right! The power of the mind is incredible!

—GRANDMA BARB

INTRODUCTION

MY MILLION-DOLLAR MONTH

In December of 2020, I made $1 million in a month.

Yes, you read that right. *One* month.

To celebrate, I did something I had always wanted to do—I bought a blue Lamborghini, my dream car. It wasn't just any Lamborghini. It was a 2021 Aventador SVJ Roadster drop-top in Cepheus blue (think the gorgeous blue of the Caribbean Sea on a sunny day).

I first dreamed of owning this car as a child, but I fixated on the dream in my early twenties and bought a toy model I placed on a shelf in my office. (I also had models of a black Mercedes-Maybach and black McLaren 600LT, two vehicles I *also* now own, but that crazy story about the power of manifestation is for a future chapter.) I wanted a car with the speed and the roar that would make me feel like I was on top of the world. Growing up poor, you do what you have to do, and you take what you can get, which is a hard way to live. If you are hungry, you eat whatever you can afford. If you need to get somewhere and all you can afford is the bus, you take the bus.

So when I went down to the dealership and drove away in my new Lambo, I felt invincible.

Superman had nothing on me.

Between my fitness business, my consulting business, and stock market profits, I had generated what I call "F-U Money." In our capitalistic society, money moves everything, and I felt there was nothing I couldn't do. F-U Money allowed me to go from doing what I could do to doing what I wanted to do. Without F-U Money, if you need a car, you have to budget, save, and settle for the most practical car. With F-U Money, you don't have to ask, "What can I afford?" You ask, "What do I want?"

Up until this point, I had been a hustler. Since seventeen, I worked constantly, with no time (or money) to give to *help* anyone else. When I hit the "million in a month" mark, I realized I finally had enough to give back. I had everything I needed and wanted, and I finally had time on my hands. I no longer needed to hustle constantly and was able to just be with friends and family and help others.

That is the premise of F-U Money: it's time you can buy. Don't want to clean your house? F-U Money lets you hire a cleaning company to do that for you. Don't want to drive around town? F-U Money lets you hire a personal driver who picks you up and drops you off whenever, wherever you want. Don't want to cook? F-U Money lets you hire a private chef who cooks all your meals for you. Want to spend more (or less) time with your kids? F-U Money gives you the means to hire whatever help you need, like a personal assistant, nanny, or au pair.

So many people (especially single mothers) work two, three, or four jobs to try and make ends meet. Without F-U Money, they can't buy time for the things that matter in life. They don't have time to work out or eat, let alone eat well. People without F-U Money don't have time to get good sleep either, so their health goes down the drain. Relationships, both personal and professional, suffer. In intimate relationships, you don't have the energy it takes to have a happy and thriving partnership (let alone have the energy for endurance in the bedroom). By the time you get home, you are exhausted, with no energy left for loved ones. In your nonromantic relationships, be that friends, family, or business, it's about more than just having negative consequences of poor health. If you have poor habits that lead to poor health, those habits will spill over into your relationships.

How you do anything is how you do everything. For example, I will not do business with overweight people. I hear you talking shit about me to your book right now. The reason is based in psychology. If you can't control what you put into your body and how you take care of your body, how can I trust that you have the right habits to take care of my money in our business deal? If you can't control your body, you can't control your mind.

I was raised by a single mother. She worked two or three jobs at a time, so she rarely made it to basketball games or our other activities. I experienced, firsthand, how my mother's lack of time impacted her relationship with my brother and me. She wasn't able to keep a relationship going either, because she spent all of her time making ends meet. The impact of her unavoidable absence wasn't instant—it was death by a thousand cuts.

What do I mean by that? As a child, I saw that lack of action was a deal-breaker that drove many of my mother's relationships apart. As an adult, I understand why the men kept leaving. Men may not want to admit it, but they do want to be loved. They want you to be available to them, for sex, sure, but just to be near them when trying to build a life together. My mom was not available because by the time she finished working her multiple jobs, she had to come home to my brother and me. They were frustrated that they were never her first (or even second) priority, which had to be work and then kids out of necessity. No man (or woman) wants to be the last priority in a relationship.

A ROADMAP TO FREEDOM

If you're reading this book, I expect I'm preaching to the choir. You *already know* you need to do something different. (You may not like what you have to do, but you'll suck it up if you really want to change.) You also *already know* you want to have more time, and to get that, you need more money. This book won't give you freedom. But it will give you a roadmap to achieve freedom—if you're willing to work for it.

A lot of people ask me, "What makes you go so hard? Why do you want to be wealthy?"

The number one reason? Options. Money gives you *options* to choose what you want.

Money equals options, which equals freedom.

I want you to have all the options you want: the *option* to be at home with your kids or hire a full-time nanny or housekeeper. If you need a car, I want you to have the *option* to drive a piece of shit or a Caribbean-Sea-blue Lamborghini. F-U Money gives you the *option* to contribute to charity or not.

This book is a roadmap to those options and, ultimately, to freedom. The first stop on that map is a look at what's stopping you from achieving that level of freedom.

What are the challenges in your life that are causing hiccups?

You need to drill down to find the issues. This requires full honesty with yourself. We all have blind spots. Maybe you're having too many kids or living beyond your means. A lot of the time, it's your actions that stop you—you are getting in your own way. Whether it's retail therapy or nonstop baby-making (you know who you are), once you know the issue, you need to figure out how to overcome it.

That's where I come in. I'll give you further insight into what F-U Money is, all the traps standing in your way of getting it, and the vehicles you can use to get you to your final destination: freedom.

The first part of the book explores the traps and everything standing between you and F-U Money. I'm talking about poppin' bottles in the club and living outside your means (among other things). How do you expect to have F-U Money when you spend everything you make on surface-level shit that doesn't matter?

Once you've had your come-to-Jesus moment and realize you're pissing away cash you could be investing, Part 2 tells you how to set your F-U Money GPS and explores different financial growth options (entrepreneurship, stocks, crypto, and real estate).

At the end of each chapter, I'll ask a question for you to explore. I've included a section for you to write down your thoughts and the actions you are going to take. No excuses. You have to be accountable to yourself, and it starts by writing down everything you need to do.

When you implement the strategies detailed in this book, getting F-U Money is possible, but before you start, you have to figure out what you really want.

Where do you want to go? What are you willing to sacrifice now for a possibility in the future?

Sit down with yourself and decide whether you want a long-term solution or a short-term gain. Then take a look at what you're currently doing and where you want to be.

What do you want? What's getting in your way? And how are you going to get it?

Some people want what they want now and are willing to give up their potential future results. You may want the Chanel handbag today, but are you okay with a generic version tomorrow? At the very beginning of your journey, these are the types of decisions you have to weigh, so it's critical to be sure of what you want.

Before you program your GPS, you need to know where to go, right? The same principle applies to your financial future. You want to be wealthy? You want to generate F-U Money? Then you need a roadmap to tell you where you need to go.

A roadmap is basically a cheat code from someone who's already taken the journey. The only person who can teach you how to generate F-U Money and become wealthy is someone who has already done it. That someone is me.

PROGRAM YOUR F-U MONEY GPS

What you're about to read isn't a get-rich-quick book, and this isn't a pyramid scheme. It isn't a feel-good read either. *F-U Principles* is going to hold you accountable and, at times, be a tough pill to swallow. There are even parts that will feel like a gut punch because F-U Money isn't easy to generate. If it were, everyone would be doing it.

My process works. I'm not fucking with you to earn a quick buck. I worked hard to earn a net worth of $2 million by the beginning of 2020. I then invested in the stock market and, as of this writing, have a net worth of $32 million. Not only that, but my roadmap has helped make at least fifteen millionaires and more than six hundred six-figure earners.

No shit. And those numbers are only climbing.

Why would I help other people make so much money? One, because I'm not an asshole. I didn't just get to the top to pull up the ladder. Two, because it feels great. It's gratifying. People who get rich shouldn't be selfish—they should give back to the community. This book is my way of helping as many people as possible make it to the top.

I've made millions and have F-U Money. Now, I'm going to teach you how to do the same. In this book, I'll show you what works, what doesn't work, what's going to get in your way, and what you can do to speed the process up. I'll show you my roadmap and what you need to do to actually travel it. I've made the mistakes, so you don't have to.

This is the book I wish my mother would have had. It could have helped her understand where to spend her money and the importance of not pissing it away on things she couldn't afford.

And who knows? If she had played her cards right, maybe she could have had her own Lambo. (But in Viola Pasifae, a deep purple, not Cepheus blue.)

Are you ready to take your first step toward the F-U Money life of your dreams? It's about time we got started because we have a whole lot of money to make.

PART ONE

F-U MONEY BASICS

When I started down this F-U Money road, my question was:

What usually stops people from getting the things they want in life?

And true to form, I didn't stop until I answered it.

I studied my environment, asked random people questions, and did my research, and I realized most people believe they can't get what they want in life because they don't have any disposable income. These are the same people who spend their money as soon as they make it and live paycheck to paycheck. They may have nice clothes and shoes and live lavish lifestyles, but their spending habits don't leave them any room for emergencies or unforeseen expenses. Then, when something out of the ordinary hits (and it always does), they're screwed—they have no extra cash, because they live paycheck to paycheck.

If this is you, you're in luck—this book will show you how to escape the paycheck-to-paycheck lifestyle. I have personally done every F-U Money lesson and skill I am going to share with you. I've also shared these F-U Money lessons and skills with others. You may not like what needs to be done, because it will be very uncomfortable, but the alternative is to stay where you are, living paycheck to paycheck.

Is that why you're here?

No!

You're here to learn how to generate F-U Money!

Getting F-U Money ready doesn't have to be hard. Let's dive into the basics.

1

WHAT IS F-U MONEY?

SO, WHAT'S F-U MONEY, ANYWAY?

F-U Money is about options, not the amount of money you have.

F-U Money isn't a number—it's a lifestyle. It's something you achieve, and you know you've achieved it based on how you are able to live. What does that mean? Think about it in terms of paradise. Your goal is to get to F-U Money paradise. You plan the vacation, you take the flight, you check into the hotel, and when you unpack your suitcase, you've made it. When you travel to paradise (a.k.a. do what you want to accomplish), and you reach that place, you've achieved F-U Money.

Let's look at an example: homelessness. There are a lot of starving and homeless people out on the streets, and you hate that. You want to say F-U to homelessness. When you get to the point that you have enough money to start getting people off the street and into a home—without skimping on bills or going into debt—you have reached *your* level of F-U Money.

F-U Money will look different for everybody because we all have a different reason why we want it—we all have something different to say F-U to. When we can achieve our goals, work on our terms, and do what we want to do *when* we want to do it, that's F-U Money.

You don't have to be an entrepreneur or a stock trader to generate F-U Money. You may enjoy your job, and if that's the case, good for you. However, you may also like buying expensive things. For you, F-U Money might mean being able to do the job you love while also having the money to buy all the nice things you want. Or F-U Money may mean hiring someone to do the work you hate, like having a personal assistant to deal with your emails, phone calls, and text messages, so you're free to spend more time doing the things you love.

For me, F-U Money meant being able to live abundantly. I wanted to be able to get up in the morning and buy whatever I wanted. Growing up poor, I had to think carefully about every single penny I spent. The idea of having F-U Money got me out of bed every morning. I was driven to make enough money to buy the things I wanted *without* worrying about whether or not I could pay my bills afterward.

Before we go any further, I want you to read this next part very carefully.

Many people tell me, "Oh Tay. If I had all that money, I'd just give it away."

Bullshit.

Yeah, I said *bullshit.*

If that's truly what you want to do, why aren't you making that amount of money already? The honest answer is that the idea doesn't excite you enough to get out of bed. Giving the money away doesn't excite you enough to do all the things you have to do to make enough money to do that. If you're just going to give all of your money away, why the fuck would you do the hard work you need to do to get it?

You wouldn't, so instead you stay right where you are and continue to blow hot air out your ass. Saying you would give all the money away is a cop-out. It's the excuse you make for why you don't already have F-U Money. It's also something you tell yourself to feel good about not having it.

This isn't the only cop-out I hear. Another popular one is "Money doesn't buy happiness."

Well, I'm pretty fucking rich, and guess what! I'm pretty damn happy.

You tell yourself this to convince yourself you don't need money to be happy because you don't have it. It's cognitive dissonance. You believe it because it justifies the decisions you've made in your life.

Don't cop out on why you want F-U Money. Really think about what you want and what will make you excited. It's okay to be selfish when you think about this. If you aren't excited to get out of bed and work for your goal, you'll never reach it.

Don't get me wrong, charity is great. It's important. I'm always happy to donate and give back. But that's not what gets me out of bed in the morning.

You aren't going to give up instant gratification if you are giving up something you want in order to just give it away later.

THE DAY I MADE IT TO F-U MONEY

I was twenty-six.

But let me back up and give you a little context. Every day, I have what I call a 'money minute' when I check my bank account balance (I started doing this when I was seventeen years old, and I do it to this day). One day when I was taking a break from running my businesses to do my money minute, a profound feeling came over me. I realized all my bills were paid. I didn't have any debt. *And I still had money left over.* This was when I realized I had F-U Money and the freedom that comes along with it. I could start having a little fun and do what I wanted to do. I wasn't quite at a million dollars a year *yet*, but I was getting close. The exact number didn't matter. What mattered was that I had finally found *freedom*.

But it was still too soon to celebrate. I didn't go out and buy my dream car. I didn't want to blow the freedom I had worked so hard for with a single purchase. Instead, I waited. I continued to drive my 2010 Toyota Camry and live with my roommate. I kept my bills as small as possible. The next year when I finally reached a million dollars? I splurged—and upgraded to a *new* Toyota Camry.

Instead of spending, I focused on the power of compound interest. I was diligent, I waited, and three years later, when I made a million dollars in a month, that's when I decided to celebrate—I bought my dream car, the Cepheus blue Lamborghini.

WEALTHY VERSUS RICH

What's the difference between being wealthy and being rich? Rich is being able to buy the things you want in *place* of the things you *need*. You need a car, but you have enough to buy a Lamborghini. You need a roof over your head, but you have enough to buy a penthouse condo or mansion. The problem with being rich is that you can stop being rich. You can be rich today and broke tomorrow.

People who are wealthy constantly create money. Their money works for them, and it lasts generations. Being wealthy means you're able to cover your lifestyle *and* your needs—you're able to live, eat, and *enjoy* a decent life. If your lifestyle needs $10,000 a month, and you have a business or asset that can kick you out $10,000 a month passively, whether you work for it *or* stay in bed all month, *that's* being wealthy.

ARE YOU ONE TRAGEDY AWAY FROM BANKRUPTCY?

This is a major problem that affects the majority of people. The most common response I hear to this topic is "Just increase the minimum wage." Yes, of course, the minimum wage should be increased—but that's also a slippery slope. Increasing the minimum wage basically tells people, "Hey, just stay here for the rest of your life." That's not the goal. The goal is not for you to live with a minimum-wage job forever. A minimum-wage job is not meant to be a career or a lifelong obligation.

When I was a teenager, I worked a minimum-wage job just like most people. I realized right away: it was not enough money. Say you work at McDonald's, and you get a pay increase. Know how much that will be? About fifteen cents. Good luck buying a Lamborghini with that.

The biggest problem with working a minimum-wage job is that when people get a pay increase—or even if they get a better job—they instantly upgrade their lifestyle. That is *not* what a pay increase is made for. Pissing away your extra money won't get you ahead. Say you get an increase and a bonus, so you get your kid that dog they've always wanted. Not only did you throw away that bonus, but you gave yourself an expense for the next ten to twenty years, depending on how long that dog lives. You have to give up something to get something, and you just gave away money you could have invested.

SINGLE-MOM DIFFICULTIES

I get it. People today are broke. It's only gotten worse over the last few years (F-U, COVID)—and it's even worse for single moms.

Single moms have a few issues on their hands. We talked earlier about how you either have time or money. Single moms are one of the few groups of people that are closest to being able to justify why they don't have enough money *or* time. This puts them in a hard situation because they're scattered—they're either trying to find ways to get more money in order to buy more time or trying to figure out how they can work more hours to make more money. The result is a lack of time, which means paying more for childcare and less money in their pocket (because childcare costs are fucking ridiculous).

I know this sounds like an impossible situation. It's not...but you might not like the answer.

The best thing that single moms can do is to team up with other single moms. Find three other single moms, and buy a house or rent an apartment together. Create your own mini-community. Once everyone lives together, you can split the bills and childcare.

In fact, the best thing to do is have one of you stay home with the kids. The other three can pay the stay-at-home mom to watch the kids while they work. The stay-at-home mom can also take care of the house, cooking, and cleaning and still get paid a living wage. Because you're splitting the bills and childcare, all of you should be able to start saving. And after saving comes investing. (More on that in Part 2.). This is your start to F-U Money.

This sounds like a radical idea. It's not. It's something people have done for generations—this idea is still practiced in other countries. The only difference is that instead of living with your parents or siblings, you're living with friends and making your own family.

DEALING WITH UNLIVABLE LIVING CONDITIONS

I get that you don't want to share a home forever. You may not be a single mom, and sharing a house is the exact situation you want F-U Money to get out of. However, you have to sacrifice to make that F-U Money.

Stretching your money to get your own place before you have F-U Money is creating an unlivable condition. You are forcing yourself to live beyond your means. True unlivable conditions are any conditions where you stretch yourself too thin trying to move somewhere or have a lifestyle you can't afford.

I once had a single-mom client who lived in LA with two kids and made $80,000 a year. Sounds like a lot, but you cannot live in LA, with two children, for that amount of money. That's unlivable. It's already hard enough to live on $80,000 a year with one kid, and when you add in that she lives in one of the most expensive cities in the country, it's no wonder she couldn't make it to F-U Money. What she *should* have done was live with three other single mothers who all made $80,000 as well. That's enough money to live on in LA and *still* be able to save enough to invest.

This is a come-to-Jesus moment—it's accountability. Why do you think you should be able to live by yourself if you've just finished your third can of tuna fish this week? If you can't afford your electricity bill this month because you just *had* to live by yourself, you need to take a long, hard look in the mirror. This suffering is unnecessary. It's also a short-term 'gain' holding you back from what you really want.

LET'S SEE IT IN NUMBERS

Let's look at the $80,000 scenario again. On the left is our single mother trying to live by herself in LA with two kids. She needs a two-bed, one-bath home. On the right is our single mother living with three other single mothers, with a total of six kids between them. If the kids share bedrooms, they need a five-bedroom house. All of these numbers are per year.

	BUDGET 1	BUDGET 2
Income	$80,000	$240,000 ($80,000 per mom)
Rent	$30,000	$80,000 ($20,000 per mom)
Childcare	$30,000 ($15,000 per kid)	$40,000 ($13,400 per mom)
Utilities and Food	$24,000	$70,000 ($17,500 per mom)
Investment Money	−$4,000	$50,000 ($12,500 per mom)

The single mother living alone ends up in the negative, living on credit cards or paycheck to paycheck. The four mothers living together, however, are earning $240,000 collectively, with three of the mothers working and one staying at home to watch the kids.

The three working mothers agree to pay for housing for everyone, which is $80,000 total. This leaves them $160,000. They then pay the stay-at-home mother $40,000, leaving all four women $40,000 each to split the utilities and food bills, which is about $70,000 total for all twelve of them (moms and kids). That means the women have a collective $90,000 a year remaining to save and invest, or even hire an assistant to help the stay-at-home mom manage the kids.

In just five years of this living situation, investing $90,000 a year at a 10 percent annual return gives these mothers over $540,000. In ten years, this family of twelve has over $1.4 million. And I do mean family. By this time, they should be a solid family. By year ten, if they decide to split the money and go their separate ways, each household of three walks away with over $360,000. Assume the average mother in this situation was thirty-five when they started. By forty-six, each single mother would have $360,000. How many forty-six-year-old single mothers have $360,000 set aside to live on and further invest? I think it's safe to say not many.

(And just think, this doesn't even take into account splitting the appreciation and sale of the house! In the LA area, a million-dollar home would double in value over ten years. That could pay off the house and leave *at least* $1 million to split between them.)

TIPS FROM TAY

I want you to write down what F-U Money would like for you and your lifestyle. Don't leave anything out! I want you to live your *best* life. What would that look like? How much money would you really need? These are important questions to answer.

Now that you have that done, write a list of the things you think are holding you back currently.

Last, make a list of the actions you are currently taking to get to the F-U Money promised land.

2

DEAL WITH YOUR DEBT FIRST

LEARNING ABOUT DEBT FROM MY MOTHER

How you do anything is how you do everything.

I learned all about bad debt from my mother—and basically everyone around me. They were taking out debt to get a new car, a new cell phone, or the latest new gadget, something that was going to depreciate and not bring in any long-term income. I watched my mom go down this slippery slope of consumerism to where she would say, "Hey, I don't have the money, but I really want this new cell phone. I don't have the money, but I really want this new car that's coming out." What ended up happening is we couldn't eat.

My mom practiced "robbing Peter to pay Paul." It really showed me what not to do, but it also showed me how uninformed and ill-equipped many people are when it comes to money. We don't really have any information when it comes to making money or even just managing money. The education is not there. As a child, you don't know what to say. As a child, I wasn't thinking, *Oh, my mom doesn't have the money education she needs.* I would think, *Wow, my mom really doesn't know what she is doing. She's really lost.* Now, I know she was doing her best. She didn't know any other way to do it.

It really confirmed for me that I wanted to do it another way. I would think, *Wow, there's gotta be a better way. There's gotta be something out there. Everybody doesn't live like this. So what are other people doing that my mom isn't?* This is what made me really start searching for answers.

My mom eventually declared bankruptcy. And ten years later, she ended up filing for bankruptcy again. That goes to show it's not necessarily about a clean slate. The real problem is the person themselves. My mom's problem was a lack of financial education. She lived well above her means. When the new cell phone came out, she had to have it. She was going to have that cell phone one way or another. She never wanted to have a roommate. She wasn't disciplined, which is one of the reasons I became extremely disciplined. I was not going to make the same mistakes. (I'd make my own, but we'll talk about those later.)

To illustrate this, one day, when I'm about nineteen, my mom comes to me and says, "Hey Tay, I need $1,000. I'm a bit behind on bills, and the money will help me get through to next month."

Now, I'm barely making it at this time. I'm trying to build my business and level up. But I say, "Hey Mom, no problem." I find the $1,000 and give it to her, saying, "Hey, that was my last thousand. So, take care of it." The next week, I take my mom out to lunch so we can hang out, and I notice she has a new cell phone. I ask, "Hey Ma, how'd you get that phone? I thought you needed money for rent. I thought you were behind." She goes, "Oh yeah. But that rent will be okay. I really wanted this phone." I could have made much better use of that money than buying a phone. But this is how she was: brainwashed by consumerism.

START WITH RADICAL ACCOUNTABILITY

I'm not sure my mom ever learned this, but the first thing you need to know is the importance of accountability.

This is going to make you uncomfortable. That's okay. Sit with it. Feel it.

No matter what happens in life, it's your fault.

Read it again.

No matter what happens in life, it's your fault.

Good or bad, everything that happens is *always* your fault.

Why do I say that?

As poor people, we blame everything (bad or good) on outside forces. I used to do it all the time. If a day went well, I'd say, "Thank Jesus." If the day was bad, I'd say, "The devil is working today." I'm not saying to stop believing in religion. What I want you to understand is that at the end of the day, your religion, your spirituality, or *whatever* you believe in puts the power and control in your hands.

If you wake up angry, it's your choice. You decided to be angry today.

If you are late for work, it's not because traffic was bad. You didn't leave enough time; you didn't check the GPS to see how long it would take to get to work that day, so it's your fault. Even if you are in a car wreck because someone else hit you, it's your fault—if you had left a few minutes earlier, you wouldn't have even been at the light to be rear-ended.

I'm talking about radical accountability.

Why is this so important? Look at any job, at any structural level. When it comes to the financial hierarchy, the person with the most responsibility makes the most money. The person at the bottom, who's doing the work, doesn't make a lot of money, because they don't have a lot of responsibilities. They show up and do a job. More money is made when someone becomes responsible for more.

Never underestimate the importance of mindset.

It's dressing for the job you want. If you show up to work in jeans and T-shirt because you're not doing an important job, you'll continue doing a nonimportant job. If you want the job where you have to wear a suit and use a briefcase, you need to start wearing a suit and carrying a briefcase. When you start dressing the part, you start acting differently, moving differently, talking differently. It's radical accountability. So if you don't make more money and you remain forever in debt (like my mom), you know it's because you didn't get off your ass and do something about it. You can't blame that on anyone else. And so, you start taking action. No matter what happens, you made the decision, so the end result is your fault—good or bad.

HOW TO DEAL WITH YOUR DEBT

Before you can start to earn F-U Money, you need to first be accountable for your debt and then deal with it. There are two ways you can handle it. The first way is the Dave Ramsey way: pay it off slowly, one day, one month, one *year* at a time.

I'll be honest and tell you, I don't recommend this strategy. Most people are so deep in debt that if they try to scrimp and save their way to paying it off, it's going to take them twenty, thirty, or even *forty* years. To top it all off, you aren't investing while doing that, and you'll never make it to F-U Money.

The second way is the way that *I* got out of debt. That's right, me, a multimillionaire once had $40,000 in debt. To start, I only paid the minimum amount due every month. Instead of putting my extra money each month toward my debt, I invested it in stages.

First, I invested $5,000 in business coaching. I was still building my fitness empire, and I knew I needed help to get to the next level. While I had $5,000 saved up, I learned from Robert Kiyosaki, author of *Rich Dad, Poor Dad*, that we use Other People's Money. Instead, I took a loan out for $10,000 (yes, more debt), hired my coach—who cost $5,000—and spent the other $5,000 on what my coach told me would help grow my business. And grow it did: I went from making $5,000 a month to making $15,000 a month.

You might be saying, "Great, Tay. Now you started paying off your debt, right?" No, not yet. I was still paying the minimum. Instead, I took the extra money I was making and reinvested it back into my business. Over the next year and a half, that reinvestment took me from $15,000 a month to $25,000 a month. Two years after I started, I only owed around $20,000 because I had still made the minimum payment each month of about $500. Now that I was making $25,000 a month, I could pay off all of my bad debt with one month's salary.

Yes, bad debt. That implies there is good debt, right? There is. Some debt is good, and you should take it out. To this day, I continue to take out good debt because it continues to help me make more money.

THE DEBT SNOWBALL

When you start accumulating bad debt, it's a snowball effect. You already couldn't afford it, so you borrow the money, and then you can't afford it even more—six months from now, a year from now, or two years from now. It was something that I saw happen with my mom because not only could she not afford the principle of the debt that she was taking out, but all debt has interest rates.

When you take out bad debt, and you couldn't afford that money to begin with, it snowballs in a bad way, and you get a bad snowball. Think of a gross, dirty, black ice ball. That's your bad debt. It's small to begin with, but when you push it down the hill, it keeps growing to a giant, black, disgusting snowball that runs you off the road.

Good debt snowballs in the opposite direction. With good debt, you take out a loan to get something that is going to make you money. That asset then pays off the debt—and still continues to make you money after the debt is paid off. Then, because you have a fully paid-for asset with no debt, you have collateral to get more good debt at a better rate, and your clean, beautiful, money-making snowball can continue to grow and bring you more money.

BAD DEBT

The more bad debt you accumulate, the harder it is to climb out of that hole—which means the longer it'll take you to get to F-U

Money. The more debt you have, the less money you have to put toward assets. Now, we all make mistakes. However, when you continue to pile on bad debt, that's when the snowball really takes off. You're already in debt, but you think you really need another loan to get that specific car.

The worst part of bad debt is that there comes a time that you get so far in the debt bubble that you go, "You know what? This is just how life is. I'm going to stay right here. This is just part of life." And you start selling yourself this dream that this is how life is always going to be. It's a type of Stockholm syndrome. You think, *This is not a good situation, but I'm going to make the best of it. In fact, I'm going to fall in love with it.* Debt is perpetual in our culture. We borrow our way to the next day.

I need you to understand that this is *not* what life has to be.

GOOD DEBT

Good debt is when you borrow money and use that money to either get something that will make more money or to get a skill that will make you more money. Now, the skill way is a thin line. Going to college is gaining a skill, but the ROI on that is not always as good as you think it will be. People end up in college debt for decades.

With good debt, whatever you do that is making you money pays off the debt. You don't pay off the debt; the thing you bought (whether a skill or asset) pays for you.

For example, say you get a loan to buy a $20,000 car. You can put that car on Turo, which lets someone rent out your car and makes you money. A $20,000 loan over five years is about $500 a month. If you rent it out for $100 a day, all you need is seven days to make that debt make sense. That car is now paying for itself, and the other twenty-three days of the month, you have a free car to drive.

TIPS FROM TAY

When you agree to take on radical accountability, you'll realize that no one is coming to save you. This instantly shifts your brain into a "let me get my shit together" mode, making your future action more intentional by default.

Bad debt slows or even stops the growth of your net worth, while good debt can supercharge the growth of your net worth. Write down a list of all your debts, good and bad.

Make a big effort to at least pay the minimums on your debts to get rid of the bad debt, and eliminate the use of debt to buy liabilities such as cars and clothes. Don't live on your credit cards!

Work toward getting your credit score over 650 and your yearly *reported* income over \$40,000. Reported is the key word there. Cash that you make and don't report to the IRS can't be counted as income when someone is looking at your credit-worthiness. It also shows you are a liar and willing to cheat the IRS. It makes the loaner wonder: *if you will cheat the IRS, will you cheat me as well?* Remember, how you do anything is how you do everything.

Once you become creditworthy enough, get funding to invest in knowledge to better yourself. Then apply that knowledge to make more money and continue the cycle.

3

IN-HOUSE ASS

LIFE WITHOUT IN-HOUSE ASS

People who go to the club are clubbing themselves over the head.

I have a good friend, Frank, who doesn't have in-house ass, and it affects his whole life.

In-house ass is the ass you are committed to. It's your partner. Instead of wasting resources chasing sex and restarting the process over and over, you stay with your one person. The more people you have to juggle, the more time you lose, and the longer it takes to get to F-U Money.

The biggest benefit of in-house ass is that you don't have to work *alone* to get to your goal. When you're single, everything is on you. You have to do all the jobs: the literal job that earns money to pay for everything, the cooking, the cleaning, the laundry, the childcare pickup. When you have a partner, however, you have someone to split the work with. You can say, "Hey, I've got dinner, you do the laundry, and we can meet back here." In-house ass becomes the thing that helps you get closer to your goal because two heads are better than one.

When Frank comes home from work, he has to do everything by himself. He has to cook, do the dishes, do the laundry, clean the bathrooms, vacuum the floors, and do all of the other chores by himself. When he wakes up in the morning, he has to make sure his whole getting-ready practice is ready: making breakfast, making sure his day is scheduled, etc. Frank doesn't have anyone to help keep him on his game. He has no extra helping hand. I've always been a believer that two sets of hands are better than one, and Frank only has one set of hands.

Even though he doesn't have a partnership, he still wants companionship. Frank is splitting his time between his business and other activities to find outside ass because he doesn't have in-house ass. He's spending money and spending time courting women, trying to close the deal.

He also has to deal with the emotional side of chasing women. When you don't have someone in-house and you are chasing new women, you are emotionally unavailable. Let's be honest: we don't trust new people we've just met. So Frank has to watch and think about every new person he talks to. They're taking up real estate in his head. *Is she really who she says she is?*

If we look at two men who are working toward F-U Money, and one has in-house ass and one does not, the one who does not have a partnership is going to struggle because he is split. His emotions, time, and money are all split. He'll constantly be thinking about where his next ass is coming from. While man number two is trying to find ass, the first man is getting more work done and making more money. Plus, he has a partner to work with in order to accomplish even more.

I have in-house ass, and it enables me to maneuver through life easier than Frank. I face the same challenges he does, but I have help. For instance, while writing this book, when I got up in the morning, I only had to get myself ready, and my woman would take care of the rest of the morning chores, such as having breakfast ready when I was done writing. Frank, on the other hand, also gets up and starts writing, but while he's writing, he's thinking, *What am I going to eat after this?* Because he doesn't have a partner, he has to figure out his food situation himself. Having a partner means I have better clarity when working. I'm never worried about anything other than the task at hand, which gives me a leg up.

I also don't have to waste time chasing ass—it's right there beside me. It's also important to like the ass sitting beside you. Not just on a physical level, but a mental and emotional level as well. If not, then your in-house ass can become more problematic than chasing it. As important as in-house is for leveling up your game, having the right ass for your partnership is even more important.

If you are working toward F-U Money, a partnership is very helpful to getting you to the F-U Money position and *staying* there. A small caveat: the only time not having in-house ass works is when you already have F-U Money. Say you were married, and the marriage helped you get to F-U Money because you were focused. But after reaching F-U Money, things went sideways, and you split. Now that you are single, things might be easier. Why? Because all the things we talked about that a partnership can help you with, you can now buy. Where's my next meal going to come from? Well, I'll just hire a chef. Who's going to clean up the house? I don't have time to do my business and clean. Guess what! I can hire a cleaner. F-U Money allows you to put all these things in place so you don't have to worry about it. (Plus, when you have F-U Money, you don't have to chase ass. It'll flow right to you.)

KEEP YOUR FUCKING PANTS ON

You don't need to chase ass until you've reached F-U Money, because it gives you a false sense of success. It makes you think things are great or at least that things are comfortable. When you aren't where you want to be (or even if you're in a bad situation), but you're still getting sex, that's a biological message to your body: *okay, I actually have it together*. Because there wouldn't be people having sex with you if you didn't have it together, right?

(If you want to see a man make a $1 million fast, tell him he can't have sex until he makes it. Watch how fast he makes that coin. It'll give you whiplash.)

Sex doesn't just make you feel comfortable. It takes up either your time or your money. To get to the act of sex, typically you have to go to dinner and wine and dine. You have to build up to the act and get your partner excited about having sex with you. This means you're wasting money you could be investing. Instead of putting more of it into your stock portfolio, you're spending your hard-earned cash on a Chanel purse.

If you don't have a lot of money, you have to give your time. You need to hang out, watch movies, and make dinner together. That's time you could be using to grow the money you do have and get to the next level.

Chasing new tail, over and over again, takes up a lot of money or time. What you really want is in-house ass.

WHY THE FUCK ARE YOU CELEBRATING?

Guess what! If you're reading this book, you haven't earned the right to chase ass. You also haven't earned the right to drink, smoke, or celebrate. You might as well say, "Hey, I haven't reached my goals yet, but let's smoke, drink, and party, because I'm on my way up."

Why don't you just throw your money into the trash?

Money is a tool for you to use: to better your lifestyle, better your happiness, etc. If you're smoking it, drinking it, or partying it away, then that money isn't contributing to the betterment of your lifestyle.

Smoking is unhealthy, but you're putting money on it. It's not good for you to drink—it's attacking your liver—but you're putting money on it. (Don't give me that, "Oh, wine is good for you!" bullshit. I was a trainer; I know the truth. It's good for you...if you drink only four ounces a month.) With all of these things, you are spending money to hurt yourself. You are saying, "Let me pay to hurt myself." If you were in a footrace, you'd be saying, "I'll give you money to take one of my legs away."

DRINKING TO RELAX

Look, I get it. Sometimes, you drink to celebrate a big event in your life or your family's life. That's not what we are talking about here. We're talking about drinking regularly to relax. Drinking to relax means you can take your mind off whatever is going on in your life. Drinking to celebrate is one thing, but it's also something I see during *depressing* times of life, when things aren't going great.

As a teenager, I worked at a grocery store, and I noticed that when there was a down economy or a recession, alcohol sales went up.

"Life's shit. Let's drink."

"Might as well get a drink and forget about it."

"A drink will help me ease the pain."

For those of us who drink to lift our spirits, we need to change our relationship with alcohol. It should be celebratory and *occasional*. Drinking can hinder you and stop you from reaching your goals. Alcohol dries out the body by drying out the blood vessels. When you drink, your blood vessels are constricted (because they're dry), so blood doesn't flow where it needs to—including to your brain. Without adequate blood flow to your brain, you can't think as well as you normally would, which impacts your money-making performance.

Then, there's how long it takes to recover. The day after you drink, you feel like shit. And depending on how much you drank, the day after that is probably a wash too. Meaning you lost two productive days trying to survive your hangover. If you drink twice a week, that's four days out of the week that you lose. Now we're looking at three days of productivity from you, versus seven days of productivity from me, a nondrinker. This equates to sixteen days a month and almost half a year of wasted time.

Who do you think is going to make more money? Who is going to get to F-U Money faster? Me, working seven days a week, or you, working three?

I can hear some of you talking shit to the book right now.

"I do it all the time."

Sure you do. But it's *not sustainable*. You can't lie to yourself forever; you know for a fact your drinking habit isn't optimal. You're doing it, yeah, but are you being the best version of yourself? You need to be that person in order to get to the next level and make all of the F-U Money you want.

There's a saying I used to hear growing up: when you go to the club, you're clubbing yourself. "Club" is a verb meaning to hit someone over the head with a blunt instrument. It's something you do to knock somebody out and take them off of their path—to keep them from getting to their destination. When you go "clubbing" (meaning you go to the club), you are clubbing *yourself* over the head. You're slowing yourself down, if not totally taking yourself out of the game, because when you go to the club, you wreck yourself—you spend all your money, and you sleep the whole next day (or two) to recover.

If you want to blow off some steam, why not do it in a healthy way? Instead of going to the dance club, go to the *exercise* club. Do something physical. When you push yourself to do a hard exercise, it creates a challenge. If I wake up in the morning and work out really hard, nine times out of ten, that's the *hardest* part of my day. Then, no matter what happens, the rest of the day is easy because I already handled the hardest thing I have to do.

For instance, on leg days, I do thirty lunges while holding my body weight. That means if I weigh 220 pounds, I have to pick up two 110-pound dumbbells and hold them while I lunge thirty times. While I lunge, I'm thinking, *Well, this fucking sucks.* But when it's done, the hardest part of my day is done. After that,

I can get an email from a disgruntled client or a nasty phone call, and I'll think, *Well, it could be that 220 pounds again that I lunged this morning, but it's not, so I'll take it.* The rest of my day is chill by comparison.

GET THAT CIGAR OUT OF YOUR GODDAMN MOUTH

Smoking cigars is something people do to celebrate. But some of you smoke cigars all the time. You should be saving celebratory things for celebrations *only*. It's something you should do when you close a business deal, when you just made really good money, or when your sister has a baby. When you sit down and smoke your cigar, and you *haven't* closed the business deal (or when nothing celebratory has happened), a signal is sent to your body that says, "Hey, life isn't so bad," and it slows you down mentally. When you do these small celebrations, you start telling yourself that life is good, because if it wasn't, you wouldn't be here smoking this cigar. With every puff, you trick your mind into thinking you've made it when you haven't.

This doesn't just apply to cigars; it applies to weed too. Not only are you tricking your brain into thinking you're comfortable, but smoking weed all the time will also cost you a lot of money. Say that dime bag of weed costs $100 and lasts you a week. You're now paying $400 a month to slow down your thinking. Instead of investing $400 a month, you're smoking it.

The same thing goes for cigarettes. How much money are you spending on those Marlboro Reds and Newport Menthols? If a pack of cigarettes costs you $10, and you smoke a pack a day, that's $70 a week, and more than $3,600 a year.

You might as well light a Benjamin on fire and smoke that instead.

Smoke costs you in the long run because a lot of people who smoke end up taxing their lungs and overall body system. It also affects your endurance, both physically and mentally. It gives you a handicap. It's putting yourself in a hard place and then trying to get yourself back out of it. Smoking also puts a lot of wear and tear on your body—and you only get one body.

IT'S TIME TO DELAY GRATIFICATION

The big thing that drinking, clubbing, smoking, and sex have in common is that they all represent instant instead of delayed gratification.

Don't waste your money on smokes, booze, or ass when you could be investing it. If you delay your fun and gratification *now* and put it toward your future, you can do things nobody else can do.

For me, my love is cars. However, instead of buying a $30,000, $40,000, or even a *$60,000* car, I continued to drive the same $15,000 car for *years*. Sure, I could have bought a more expensive car years before I did, but I delayed gratification and instead put that money into my investments. That's why, seven years down the road, I was able to go buy my $700,000 dream car instead of settling for a good car.

So, put down that drink, put out that cigar, and cancel that date. Focus on what you really, really want—refer back to your answers at the end of Chapter 1—and understand that everything else is a distraction from that goal.

TIPS FROM TAY

Are you delaying gratification?

What are you wasting money and/or time on that you could be investing for the future?

_____

_____

_____

_____

4

COMPOUND YOUR COMFORT

THE SWITCH FROM TIME TO MONEY

Why not go extra hard today so you can enjoy tomorrow?

When I was nineteen and working at the warehouse, I realized how much time it was taking from me. I lived an hour away from the job, then worked nine to ten hours, then commuted another hour home. That was thirteen, fourteen, sometimes *fifteen* hours taken from my day for this job. Then, by the time I got my food and ate it, it was time to go to bed. After eight hours of sleep, it was time to go back. At this point I realized I was out of time.

Now, when it comes to common sense, I'm overly common. I simplify everything. *I'm not making as much money as I want to make, and I don't have time to go get another job*, I thought. *What can I do?* I knew I had a few options. I could sleep less, I could find a way to get a raise at my job, or I had to find something to replace that job that would make more money per hour. (Work smarter, not harder.)

My work at the warehouse was hard physical labor, so I couldn't take away sleep. I needed seven or eight hours a night at minimum. I wanted to quit, but quitting is hard for me, so what I did was bring it into fruition. I started talking about needing to leave the job. Then, when I was on vacation at Disney World with a friend, I decided to take an extra day of vacation, and they ended up firing me. It was a blessing in disguise because I was able to find a job that was going to pay me more for my time, and as we know, I ended up going into entrepreneurship. I was only making twenty-five dollars an hour at the warehouse, and I started making a hundred an hour with my fitness business. This not only gave me more time in my day, but it also increased how much money I could bring in within that same amount of time.

It was at this point, age twenty-two, that I started to learn that time is more valuable than money—much more valuable. This is when I started to ask myself, "How much time is this going to cost me?" I started budgeting by time rather than money. For instance, I need to hire someone to clean the house, so I ask a friend for a recommendation, and they say it's going to cost $300. Great, I can make that in ten minutes. It's worth it for me to spend the $300 rather than spending three hours myself to clean it. Most people are money focused instead of time focused. They would rather save the $300 and clean their house themselves.

The reason why is a mental byproduct of the way our professional system works in the United States. The nine-to-five mode makes people think of time in terms of their current hourly wage. Say I ruin my white sneakers. If I have to go buy another pair of hundred-dollar shoes and I make ten bucks an hour, that's going to cost me ten of my hours. (Side note: if you're making ten bucks an hour, you have no reason to be buying hundred-dollar shoes. That's called overspending. If you have to say, "Oh, I can't buy another one of those because it costs too much," then you spent too much on it.)

YOU EITHER HAVE TIME OR MONEY

People have two resources they can use: time or money. Everything takes resources. If you don't have the money to buy the resource, you have to put in the time to get it. If you don't have the time to get the resource (because you are using the time to make money), you need to sacrifice money to buy it. And if you don't have either? You have a bigger fucking problem.

If you think you don't have time or money, you're wrong. You say you don't have time because you are always working. Then, where's your money? The answer (that you don't want to admit): going down the drain as you spend it lavishly and irresponsibly. When you spend money like that, you're also wasting your time because you are just throwing the value of that time away.

Or you could have another type of spending problem: a *time* spending problem. Instead of shopping for things you don't need, you are spending valuable work time watching TV, going to too many parties, chasing women for sex, or sleeping too much. You get the idea.

SLEEP LESS, WORK MORE

It's time again for some brutal honesty. If you are sleeping more than seven and a half hours, you are a fucking lazy ass. Your laziness is going to stop you from getting to your goal. If you are saying, "Tay, I want to make more money—I want to get to the next level," and then you sleep eight, nine, ten hours, I'm going to respond to you, "Do you really want it?" Because your sleeping habits indicate otherwise.

There's a (good) caveat to this sleeping issue, however. If you have the built-in in-house ass, like we talked about in Chapter 3, then you have a built-in team. Both of you don't have to get up immediately after seven hours. For example, I let my lady sleep nine hours. Instead, I'll start the day off, so she can get plenty of rest. Then, in the afternoon after I've been working for hours, she's fully rested, and she can keep everything going while I take a nap.

I can hear you saying, "But Tay, I *need* my sleep. I can't function without at least ten hours of sleep." Well, I never said this would be easy. In fact, if you think back to the Introduction, I *specifically* told you this would require a lot of hard work. However, if you use the "stay down until you come up" method and sacrifice six to ten years of waking up an hour early, then ten years down the road, you can sleep as long as you fucking want to. I no longer have to set alarms. I sleep until my body tells me to wake up. That's because I sacrificed my sleep for years until I reached F-U Money.

For years, I put my business as the number one priority. In our society, men are not shit if they aren't producing. You are useless as a husband, as a father, as a basketball player, as a worker, as anything. If you don't produce, you are useless and disposable. For me, as a man who knows this, producing was my first priority. While I was sacrificing to reach F-U Money, I was not a joy to be around because no one got my full attention. My entire attention went to the business. My filter for everything I did was: Is this going to help me or hurt me? Is this going to take time or give me time? At the time, I had a girlfriend and she'd want to hang out. But that was time away from the business, so I'd constantly tell her, "No, not hanging out today." I'm a nice guy, and I'm told I'm fun to be around now, but no one was able to get anything out of me at that time because I was hyperfocused on my goal. Looking around at my cars, beachfront houses, and stock portfolio, I'd say it was worth it.

STAY DOWN UNTIL YOU COME UP

When I say stay down, it basically means, "Hey, you're broke. Stay down. Hey, you can't afford that. Stay down. Stay where you are." Over time, you'll start coming up. You'll start slowly gaining in life: gaining more time, gaining more money, gaining more resources. You're not up yet though. You're slowly going up, but for now, stay down, stay down, stay down. You'll know when you're up. You'll feel it. That's when you can come in and say, "Okay. I no longer have to stay down because I'm up." This is another way of saying live below your means.

SACRIFICE TODAY FOR COMFORT TOMORROW

This journey to F-U Money means delaying the comfort of today so we can live overly comfortable tomorrow. To explain this even further, we're going to monetize the word "comfort."

Let's say comfort costs a dollar. Everything you want to do today costs you a dollar. That can include watching Netflix, sleeping in, having extra sex, going clubbing, drinking; all of these combined cost one dollar. When I say you need to sacrifice today's comfort, what I mean is only spending fifty cents of that comfort dollar so that in two to ten years, you can spend two dollars a day. We are compounding our comfort.

Let's quantify nonproductive activities. Assume each person is given $30 a week (and keep in mind these dollars can be saved and used at later dates.)

UNPRODUCTIVE PERSON		PRODUCTIVE PERSON	
Comforts = $1 Each	Cost of comfort	Comfort Sacrifice	Cost of sacrifice
2 Hours of TV a Day	$14 (7 Days a Week × $2)	4 Hours of TV a Week	$4 (4 Hours a Week × $1
Smoking 3x a Week	$3	No Smoking	$0
Drinking Alcohol or Wine 3x a Week	$3	One Glass of Wine a Week	$1
Happy Hour or Bar/Club 2x a Week	$2	No Happy Hour or Clubbing	$0
Sleeping More than 7–8 Hours 4x a week	$4	Sleeping 6–8 Hours a Night	$0
TOTAL	$26	TOTAL	$5

At the end of the week, the unproductive person has $4 left over, while the productive person has $25 left over. After ten years of this, our unproductive person has $2,080 saved to allow for extra comforts while our productive person has $13,000 saved for extra comforts.

At this point, our productive person can sleep in and watch as much TV as they want! Now imagine thirty years of these numbers. We call that retirement. Yes, your retirement will literally be shaped by the comforts you enjoyed over the years.

EVERYTHING COSTS SOMETHING

Everything in this world costs something as far as resources. It either costs you time or money. But today, people feel a sense of entitlement. They believe they deserve something without sacrificing their time or their money. Whatever you want in life, it's going to require something of you or from you.

Many women want a man who has his shit together. Men want a pretty piece of ass. So, women, what sacrifices do you have to make to get a man with his shit together? It's going to cost you time. You have to work out. You have to put in time to do your makeup and keep your body together. It might also cost you money. You have to get your hair done. You have to spend more on food to make sure your body looks tight. These are all sacrifices you have to put in to get what you want: a man with his shit together.

But what I'm seeing today is the opposite of that. A lot of women are showing up and saying, "I deserve a good man because my dad told me I'm a fucking princess. Take me as I am. Yeah, I'm fat, I'm unhealthy, and I don't care how I look going out, but you should accept me anyway because that's what I've been told I deserve."

This is the attitude of someone that didn't, or doesn't, want to put in the work to earn what is desired. The bottom line is that energy attracts energy. When you put in the hard work and "sacrificing" energy, that same type of energy is returned to you by way of life partners, financial success, and anything else you want.

TIPS FROM TAY

In this chapter, I want you to account for every single moment in your life. I do mean everything. There are twenty-four hours in a day, so I want you to put all twenty-four hours down on a piece of paper and dedicate an action to each hour.

_____

_____

_____

_____

This makes using your time intentional. When you wake up in the morning, you know exactly what you are supposed to do each hour of the day. You might dedicate an hour to Netflix or an hour to sex, and that's fine. The purpose of this exercise is to stop you from overindulging. So, if you dedicate an hour to Netflix, when that hour is up, there's no more Netflix. You can't say, "Oh, just one more episode."

This is also a great tip if you suffer from overeating. Instead of eating chips out of the bag, put a specific amount into a bowl, put the bag away, and then eat just that bowl. Don't get up to refill. Once your bowl is empty, you are done.

5

EAT AND LIVE LIKE SHIT

IT'S TIME TO EAT THE SHIT

You are what you consume. Don't like your current situation?
Look at your consumption.

While getting my hair cut one day, my barber told me he was
looking for a new car. (Yeah, I know. It's another story about
cars. But I love cars, so deal with it.)

"What're you thinking about getting?" I asked him.

"Man, I really want this really nice Mercedes truck," he said.

"Have you looked at it yet or priced it out?"

"No, I'm going later this week."

A few weeks later when I saw him again, I asked how the car search was going. He replied that it was going well.

"Great, so you found out about the Mercedes truck? You really like it, right?" I asked.

"Well, yeah, but I think I actually want the BMW 3 Series," he said.

I'm even less subtle in person than I am in print, so I said, "Wait a fucking minute. You don't *want* a 3 Series, do you? It's just what you can afford right now."

I got on his ass and told him he was *forcing* himself to want a BMW, because it was a luxury brand he could afford. He was settling for a car he didn't really want, just to say that he had a BMW.

He was settling. Instead, he needed to eat the shit.

WHY WOULD I EAT SHIT?

Of course, I'm not talking about literally eating shit. By eating shit, I mean living uncomfortably.

Sounds terrible, right? Why would you live like that?

Because when you force yourself to eat shit and live a horrible existence, it makes you uncomfortable. And when you are uncomfortable, you work harder. You show up, more and more, because you are desperate to get out of this uncomfortable space.

One of the biggest pieces of advice I give people is to eat shit for five to ten years, and make sure you are doing something useful with that money—investing it in some way—versus making your hell hole comfortable. I see people do this all the time. They say, "Oh, I'm in a hell hole because I don't make a lot of money. But I want to make my broke-ass hell hole comfortable. I want to open up credit cards, take out loans, and make my situation worse by making it *feel* better."

PEOPLE WHO TRY TO GET RICH QUICK STAY BROKE LONGER

The people who try to get rich quick say things like, "I gotta get rich tomorrow because I hate my job, and I'm ready to quit *now*." But they don't know *when* to cut their losses because they need the money—and so they lose more than they started with.

To get rich, there are a few components that come with it. The first is time. The way the rich throttle works is: the longer timeline you give yourself, the easier it will be. The second component is risk. The less time, the more risk you have to take. When you decrease one component, you increase the other. So when you say, "I have to get rich quick," you are throttling back the time you are giving yourself, which means you have increased the risk to sky-high levels.

When you take risk that high, it means you could potentially lose all of your money—and sometimes even more than you put in. I've seen someone put in $2,000 and lose $5,000. I've seen someone who went into real estate and bought a property because it looked like a really good steal, and they thought they could flip it really quick. But the free market didn't want it, so they ended up stuck with this house, paying rent and property taxes, bleeding out money they no longer had. They ended up selling it for pennies on the dollar just to get it off their books, because it was costing them so much money.

In the investment world, a really good return is about 8 to 15 percent per year. Sounds low, but only if you don't have a lot of money. If you have $10 million invested and make a 10 percent return, that's $1 million that you earned by sitting on your ass.

What these get-rich-quick people don't understand is that every market—whether crypto, real estate, the stock market, whatever—is set based on the people with the money. So when some broke asshole tries to create an unrealistic scenario inside a market that's run by people with the money, they instantly set themselves up for failure. When these people say, "I got $10,000. How can I turn that into a million in one year?" they're asking for a 10,000 percent return.

That doesn't happen.

What *does* happen is they make it to 10 percent, maybe even to 15 percent, but they're still holding out for that *10,000* percent. Then, when the market goes against them, they start to lose money and then *continue* to lose it, still trying to get that *unrealistic* return. You cannot force 10,000 percent out of a market that's not made to return 10,000 percent. It's that simple.

Don't get me wrong. Every once in a while, people do get lucky. I've seen it. So yes, a 10,000 percent return *can* happen, but it's not something that happens every day or even every *year*. It's not something you can bank on, pun intended.

FAST FOR DISCIPLINE

Contrary to what you might think, I'm a big foodie. I love to eat. (Don't worry. I promise this isn't an out-of-left-field topic change.) But I'm also a fan of fasting. On a dime, I can decide, "Hey, no more food for the next two days." I can sit down for dinner any time during those two days, watch other people eat, and consume nothing. It requires a lot of discipline, but because I've built the right muscles, I'm able to do it.

Fasting helps build your discipline muscle. That's the first reason why I like fasting. This chapter is all about delayed gratification—about eating shit—and that requires discipline. Fasting is the ultimate way to delay gratification. If you can say no and refrain from your favorite foods, everything else is easy to say no to.

Why do I care about discipline so much—and why should you? I have always wanted to be *great*, and I have found that all of the greats are *great* because they do something that other people can't (or aren't able to) do. They are disciplined enough to keep going, when other people quit because it's "too hard."

I've had a lot of people ask me, "How are you able to have all this success? You got the cars, the money, the jewelry, and you don't cheat. How can you do all that?"

Discipline.

I associate my discipline with the result of greatness. Think of the people who are considered great. They are great because they can do something other people can't or aren't willing to do. People ask me how I have all these cars, money, jewelry, and success. Men ask me how I don't cheat. The answer is simple: disciple. I usually tell these people that they don't have what I have because they are thinking about those questions in the first place. With focus and discipline, you can achieve greatness.

To build your discipline muscle, start small. Fast in small blocks throughout the day. Start by skipping breakfast. Drink plain tea or water instead of food, and only eat inside an eight- to ten-hour window. Once you conquer that, you can skip breakfast *and* lunch. This can usually get you to a twenty- to twenty-four-hour fast. Now, you don't have to do this big of a fast every day. It can be once a week in order to give your body a break. Listen to this because it's important. Your body is constantly digesting and breaking shit down. Every day, all day, we are trying to process and break things down because we are eating and drinking too much. Too much food, too much coffee. Long fasts are a great way to give your body a much-needed break.

To build up your discipline muscles through fasting, start small. Fast in small blocks throughout the day.

- First, skip breakfast.

- Drink water (you should *always* be drinking plenty of water throughout the day), but don't eat any food.

- Then, build your way up to eating within an eight- to ten-hour window, fasting the other fourteen to sixteen hours of the day.

You don't have to start off doing this every single day of the week—start with one day, and then build up. Discipline is like any other muscle; it takes time and work to make it strong.

On a normal day, I eat all my calories within a three-hour window. If it's a really busy day or if I feel like my body needs it, I'll go thirty-six to forty-eight hours without food. For me, this frees up my mind. I don't have to worry about what I'm going to eat next, and I don't have to waste time preparing it. I follow this principle with my clothes as well. I wear a single color per outfit. Normally, it's all black. If I'm going out somewhere fancy, I'll wear all white. If I want to be colorful, I'll wear all of one color, such as an orange tracksuit. The aim is to take away the decision-making fatigue from everything in my life that is simple and that I have to do every day. *What do I want to wear today? Does this match? What should I eat?* When you have to get up and ask yourself all these questions before you even leave the house, your brain is fried from making a dozen small decisions—and you haven't even made a real decision yet that's going to impact your life or finances. Instead, by fasting, I can just wake up, shower, brush my teeth, and hit my day running.

As I mentioned earlier, fasting is also important because it gives our bodies a break. Our bodies are constantly working and breaking food down. That's a lot of extra energy! Our bodies never get a break, ever—unless we fast.

Be good to your body and give it a break so it doesn't have to work so hard and use up your extra energy, energy you could be using to get closer to F-U Money.

In Chapter 2, we discussed how strenuous exercise can help you prepare for the day ahead, because you've already done the hardest thing you'll have to do that day. But exercise also gives you physical and mental endurance, both of which are essential for helping you invest. Investing is an endurance game, and if you don't have the physical endurance, it's going to be hard to maintain the emotional, physical, mental, and spiritual endurance that comes with building a business and investing.

The human body is like a machine, and we have a choice: we can either *not* tune our machine, or we can tune our machine to be a high-performing machine. Exercise is one way to tune our machine. For example, a lot of us tend to get tired in the middle of work. "I'm ready to go home. I can't take any more. I'm tired." The reason why people get tired is they don't have the physical or mental endurance (and they probably aren't eating healthy or fasting). They aren't tuning their machine the way they need to, and then they are trying to enter a game (business and investing) that is based around competition. So, when they try to go up against me in this game, I'm going to have a way better outcome. Why? Because I'm a tuned machine. My endurance is better than yours, so I can outlast, outwork, and outthink you. All of these come from endurance, which comes from exercise.

Exercise also affects your general life sustenance. If you aren't exercising and eating right, and then go hard on your mind and body on a daily basis, your body isn't going to be able to handle it. This is why we see old men having heart attacks while having sex or while working at the office. Their heart is not conditioned to put up with everything they are trying to make it do. The last thing you want to do is make it to F-U Money and have a heart attack before you can enjoy it.

TIPS FROM TAY

For this chapter, I want you to do your homework. Find the highest-returning market (stocks, crypto, real estate, etc.) or vehicle over a five-year average. So, for instance, what has the S&P 500 stock market done over the last five years?

Then, average that out on a yearly basis.

Let's say crypto returned 500 percent over the last five years. That's 100 percent a year.

Now, look at the expectations you have on the return you expect if you flip your money. Are they realistic when you compare them to the highest-returning market you just researched?

If crypto is the highest-returning market that you researched, and it caps out at 500 percent—and you want a 10,000 percent return—then you know your expectations are unrealistic and you need to adjust them.

I also want you to start exercising. At least three times a week, I want you to do thirty minutes of some type of cardio: walking in the neighborhood, getting on a treadmill, whatever. This is *at minimum*. Ideally, you would do thirty minutes a day, but you need to build up your endurance. So, start with three times a week and build up over time.

6

STEPPING OVER DOLLARS TO SAVE PENNIES

GROWING UP LOWER CLASS

If you are born poor, it's not your fault. If you die poor, that's all on you and the decisions you made.

My first experience with the class system was when, at thirteen years old, I found out that there was a hierarchy of classes, and I realized that the way that I thought and operated was not indicative of the class I was in. I knew then that I was not supposed to be in the lower class; I was not supposed to be poor. A lot of kids are green, and the greener you are, the less aware you are of how things work for you. If you are green coming up as a child, you think that someone put you in this position and said you are meant to be poor, so you stayed there, while this lucky group of people were picked to be in the higher class.

Once you come out of that green space, you are no longer oblivious to how the class system works. Simply put, people who are in the lower class are making bad decisions, while people who are in the higher classes are making better decisions. I was very observant as a kid, and I started putting the people around me in sectors. I noticed that the people who smoked, drank, and lied a lot were in the broke sector. I realized if I didn't want to be broke, I shouldn't smoke, drink, or lie.

When you come to that conclusion, everything gets better. I came to this conclusion at thirteen when I realized that I was not supposed to be poor because I was making the right decisions in life. For instance, at thirteen, I started cutting grass. I got my mom to get me extra gas, which cost twenty dollars, and then I knocked on thirty doors until ten people let me cut their yard for twenty dollars each. I ended up bringing home six hundred dollars in a single weekend.

THE ECONOMIC CLASS SYSTEM: WHERE DO YOU FALL?

Do you know where you fall in the current US economic class system?

The 2021 poverty guidelines released by the Department of Health and Human Services explains the amount of income a person or family must be under in order to qualify as being in poverty.

PERSONS IN FAMILY/HOUSEHOLD	POVERTY GUIDELINE
1	$12,880
2	$17,420
3	$21,960
4	$26,500
5	$31,040
6	$35,580
7	$40,120
8	$44,660

For families/households with more than 8 persons, add $4,540 for each additional person.

Chart of 2021 Poverty Guidelines for the 48 Contiguous States and the District of Columbia[1]

---

1 Office of the Assistant Secretary for Planning and Evaluation (ASPE), 2021 Poverty Guidelines, accessed November 14, 2021, https://aspe.hhs.gov/topics/poverty-economic-mobility/poverty-guidelines/prior-hhs-poverty-guidelines-federal-register-references/2021-poverty-guidelines#threshholds.

Finding out if you are middle class is more complicated because knowing what class you are in varies depending on where you live. Let's look at what the thresholds are in Los Angeles, California versus Huntsville, Alabama.[2]

	LOS ANGELES, CALIFORNIA	HUNTSVILLE, ALABAMA
Lower Class	$56,799	$28,934
Middle Class	$113,599	$55,305
Upper Class	$170,400+	$155,208
Average Home Cost	$988,288	$182,900
Comfortable Cost of Living	$150,391	$42,000

All numbers are annual.

How much do you make right now? I'm guessing it's more along the lines of Alabama middle-class levels. If you want to live in Alabama, then great, you don't have to change anything you are doing. If not (and really, why would you?), it's time to start changing some things.

---

2 Erika Giovanetti, "The Salary You Need to Live Well in LA Is Staggering," GOBank-ingRates, April 5, 2019, https://www.gobankingrates.com/money/economy/salary-need-live-well-la-all-time-high/; Rotate Digital, "A Local's Guide to Cost of Living in Huntsville, AL," This Side Up Moving, December 13, 2021, https://www.thissideup-moving.com/a-locals-guide-to-cost-of-living-in-huntsville-al/; Zillow, "Los Angeles Home Values," last updated June 30, 2022, https://www.zillow.com/los-angeles-ca/home-values/; Data USA, "Huntsville, AL," accessed August 11, 2022, https://datausa.io/profile/geo/huntsville-al#economy; Los Angeles Almanac, "Middle Class in Los Angeles County," accessed August 11, 2022, http://www.laalmanac.com/employment/em720.php.

Now, I don't want you to look at these numbers and think that once you make it to $100,000, you've made it. Don't get me wrong; $100,00 is not bad. But it should *never* be the pinnacle. It's not your "I made it!" moment. It should only ever be "okay" money. It's the place you get to in order to start investing enough to make a million dollars.

If you want to be making F-U Money, you need to be closer to the top 1 percent. What's considered the top 1 percent in America? In 2018, the average annual income for the top 1 percent was $737,697, and for the top 0.1 percent, it was $2,808,104.[3]

It's important that you understand all of these numbers because if you don't, you can be manipulated. Currently, the middle class is being manipulated to think that everything is great and that they shouldn't strive to get out of it. After all, America is middle class, your grandma was middle class, and you had a great life, right? So many people are trying to push this narrative, and it's not true. Really look at the numbers. How close to poverty are you? How close to upper class are you? When you look, I think you'll realize that the bottom 1 percent of the population is just a few paychecks away from poverty.

The big secret is that the top 1 percent is also getting rocked to sleep. They're telling those people who are making $400,000 a year that they made it, that it's time to chill out, relax, coast

---

3 Julia Kagan, "How Much Income Puts You in the Top 1%, 5%, 10%?" Investopedia, last updated April 26, 2022, https://www.investopedia.com/personal-finance/how-much-income-puts-you-top-1-5-10/.

to retirement at age sixty-five or seventy, and everything will be great. However, the range in the top 1 percent is between $400,000 and $1 billion a year. So these people think they're in the club with Jeff Bezos, but they are not—at all. Remember when we talked about how smoking and drinking tells your mind to relax and that things are good? Being told you are in the 1 percent does the same thing. So to live the 1 percent lifestyle, you start hanging out, spending money you don't have, and before you know it, you go broke.

By being aware of the classes, you can be aware of where you stand, avoid getting too comfortable, and stay on your toes. You haven't made it, and life isn't over; don't get comfortable.

HAVING KIDS IS COSTING YOU F-U MONEY

You already know having kids is expensive, but it's even more shocking when you see it written down. According to the USDA, the average cost of raising a child over eighteen years for a middle-income married couple is $284,570. That's $15,809 a year. Say that couple has three kids. That's $31,618 a year. Four kids: $47,427. That doesn't even include paying for the kids' college education.[4]

---

4 Mark Lino, "The Cost of Raising a Child," U.S. Department of Agriculture (USDA), February 18, 2020, https://www.usda.gov/media/blog/2017/01/13/cost-raising-child.

And more importantly, it doesn't include money for yourself. According to the 2019 Consumer Expenditure Survey, the yearly expenses for one adult totaled $38,266.[5]

So now, if it's just you and your kid, you need to make at least $54,075. For you and two kids: $69,884. For you, a partner, and two kids, you need to make *at least* $108,150.

But if you want to make F-U Money, you need to do more than make ends meet. You need money to invest—and you need to think about the impact of inflation on your earnings.

YOUR COST OF LIVING IS CONSTANTLY CHANGING

As of the end of 2021, inflation was at 5 percent. That means every two years, you are losing 10 percent of your buying power. If you save up $10,000 over ten years, what you really end up with is $5,000 because of inflation (and that's *if* inflation doesn't get worse). That carton of organic strawberries you buy every week that costs $6? In ten years, it will cost $12. It sounds unrealistic, but it's possible because it happens a little bit at a time. A small price increase of $0.60 every year doesn't seem large, but over time, it really adds up.

---

5   U.S. Bureau of Labor Statistics, "Table 1400. Size of Consumer Unit: Annual Expenditure Means, Shares, Standard Errors, and Coefficients of Variation," in *Consumer Expenditure Survey, 2019*, accessed November 16, 2021, https://www.bls.gov/cex/tables/calendar-year/mean-item-share-average-standard-error/cu-size-2019.pdf.

You may be thinking, "Yeah, but Tay, my employer gives me an increase every year, so it's not a big deal." First, that's great *if* you have an employer that gives a yearly salary increase—not all companies do. However, that increase is usually only 1–2 percent, which is not enough to cover the inflation increase of 5 percent. The moral of this story is not only do you need to think about whether you make enough to support yourself today but also whether you are going to make enough money to support yourself tomorrow.

You may make $50,000 today, but in ten years, that could be the equivalent of $35,000. You need to come up with other streams of income to make up for these powers outside of your control. You can't change the rate of inflation—you have to ride the wave or get wiped out.

YOU CAN MAKE MORE MONEY BUT YOUR TIME IS FINITE

That doesn't mean you need to scrimp on every tiny detail to save more money. In fact, a lot of the time when we're trying to save money, we actually lose a lot more. Let's look at an example.

Say you are looking for gas, and you want to get the cheapest possible rate in order to save. You drive all over town, checking rates, and find a gas station that is twenty cents cheaper per gallon. If you have a twenty-gallon gas tank, you've saved two dollars! Great, right? Wrong. First, you put wear and tear on your car for no reason, reducing its overall life. Second, you wasted time on the search. You may have saved two dollars, but you gave up ten dollars. This is what I call stepping over dollars to save pennies.

Other terrible examples include the following:

- Making your own clothes (to save money, not if you are trying to be a fashion designer)

- Changing the brakes or oil in your car

- Cutting your grass

- Cooking your food

You find yourself researching, learning, and trying to be good enough to do ten to twenty things a week when you should be focusing on the *one* thing that's going to make you the most money.

I've always believed in tribe living. You shouldn't try to figure out the perfect way to exercise and be healthy alone. For years, I was a personal trainer, so I've trained the "tribe." I do the training to take care of you, and then others can take care of me with whatever it is they do. For instance, I have a cook in my tribe who makes the food for everyone.

There may be a person in your tribe that wants to be the stay-at-home mom and take care of the kids. Or a teacher who wants to teach the kids at home. Let them, and pay them. Then you have a chef for the tribe and a teacher for the kids. Maybe one of you wants to farm and plant produce for the tribe. If you have someone who loves to clean and make things look pretty, hire them to do that.

This is how you make all your money—focus on one thing. Stop stepping over dollars (to save pennies) by changing your own oil or cutting your own grass when there's someone right down the street who can do it for you much cheaper than what it's costing you in time.

Build a community—but build the right community. Remember, people are in their spot in life because of how they act and think. You need to build a community that doesn't have a poverty mindset. Surround yourself with people who make good decisions instead of bad decisions that put them back in poverty. You don't want people in your community who lie, don't follow through on their promises, or use others to make their own lives easier. These are the types of people who keep you poor. If your community is smoking, drinking, and lying, then you need to get out of that community and find one that is focused on growth. The right community lets you utilize your skill and leverage someone else's skill.

The only way this will work is through reciprocity. This is when you can say, "I have a skill, you have a skill, and I am going to share my skill and/or resources," and the other person will reciprocate and share their skill as well. In bad communities, people will use your skill and resources, but they won't offer anything in return. Create the right community, and you will all thrive.

PAY FOR THE SHORTCUT

Why would you take the long, hard road when you could pay for a shortcut?

"What do you mean, Tay?"

I mean pay for a coach.

Say you are starting a business, and you have no fucking clue what you're doing. You find a person who is in the exact position that you want to be in—but they want to charge you $5,000 to teach you how to get exactly where they are. They will give you the shortcut, the cheat code, to get there faster.

But you don't want to pay. You say, "Oh, no. I'm not giving you $5,000. No way. That's too much money." Instead, you try to recreate the wheel and spend ten times as long trying to figure it out on your own. Now, not only did you cost yourself time—instead of getting there in two years, it takes you ten years—but you also cost yourself money. If it takes you ten years to scale up your business to where it could have been in two years, you didn't make all the money you *could have made* in years three through ten. Being cheap up front costs you money *and* time, which makes it the most expensive option. (Go figure.) You stepped over a lot of dollars saving those pennies.

BE AWARE OF THE OPPORTUNITY COST

Before you make any decision on whether or not to do something, make sure to look at the opportunity cost. What is it going to cost you *not* to do it?

For example, I spent $5,000 on my first business coach. If I didn't spend that $5,000, I would have missed out on the $250,000 a year he helped me make. The opportunity cost there was: do I want to save $5,000, or do I want to make $250,000?

Here's another example. Many people say no to networking opportunities because they are not sociable. Before you say no, think about what the opportunity cost is. There could be five millionaires there, and three of them are looking forward to meeting you, or maybe they are interested in investing in your current project. By saying no to a networking event, you could be missing out on a thousand-dollar opportunity or a million-dollar opportunity. You never know.

For me, when it comes to anything that can be helpful to anything I'm doing in life, my answer is rarely no. Don't step over dollars to save pennies, even when those pennies are time. "Oh, I don't really feel like going out. I want to save my energy and take a nap." Okay, but you stepped over a dollar to save your time and take a nap, when you could have made a couple million dollars over the next five years by meeting the people at that event.

TIPS FROM TAY

For this chapter, I want you to figure out how much your time is worth. To be very clear, I don't want to know what *someone else* decided your hour is worth—I want your opinion. If your last job paid you $20 an hour, that's not what your hour is worth; that's how much you settled for.

This task will be difficult, especially if you've only worked hourly jobs. Whatever your background, just make sure to be honest with yourself. Not everyone is worth $1,000 an hour. Your hourly worth comes from the value you can create.

What is your value add? Value add can simply be something that you are able to provide to anything or anyone. For example, say it's raining outside, and you have on nice clothes but no umbrella. I have an umbrella, so I have value. It's that simple. So if I bring my umbrella over and cover you up, I just added value to your life. Now, you aren't going to pay me $10,000 for this value. Instead, in life, you have to scale your value and decide what it's worth.

Another example: as a personal trainer, I knew that people valued their health and their life. So, the question became "How much are they willing to pay for their life?" I started to understand that people didn't make the connection between physical fitness and their overall life, a.k.a. living. People would say, "Oh, but I can live without fitness." So I knew there was not a lot of value there because thanks to that lack of connection between fitness and life, they wouldn't pay me much. But if I could make that connection for them, they would pay me more because they didn't want to die.

That made me think... *What's something that people value more than fitness and their life?* The answer: money. Because that's what makes the world go round. It's how you eat, it's how you take care of your family, and it's how you survive. I became more invested in learning how to create value in someone's life in order to make more money. This is how I was able to move my value from $300 a month to $5,000 a month. People were willing to pay me that much money because I was creating more value.

The root of this is: if I can solve a bigger problem for you, you're willing to pay me more money. The bigger the problem I can solve, the more value I create, which means the more money I can create.

Once you know your value, every time you get ready to do something, such as cleaning your house, look at whether you can pay someone else a cheaper rate than your hourly worth. For example, say your hourly rate is $50, and you need to clean your house today. If it's going to take you three hours to clean your house, it will cost you $150. However, if you can pay someone $20 an hour to clean your house, that's a total cost of $60. At the end of those three hours, you end up being net positive $90 to let someone clean your house.

Here's another example for you. Say your value is $500 an hour, and you need to cook. You can either go cook, or you can use that hour to find somebody else to create value for, and pay someone less than $500 to cook for you. If you hire someone, you gain back that valuable hour. This becomes even more important when you start getting pulled at different ends. "I don't have time for my kids. My wife is fucking pissed because I'm not spending enough time with her." When those things start to happen, you realize that your time is more valuable than cutting grass. If your wife is complaining that you don't spend enough time with her, fuck that grass. Go spend time with her and pay someone else to cut the grass.

If there is a way to save money by not doing something you're currently doing, you should do it. Hire someone else to clean your house, wash your car, or really anything you don't like doing. Even if you just break even paying someone to do it, you should still hire them. Why? Because it will increase your quality of life and make you more money indirectly. If your hour is worth $1,000, and you pay someone $1,000 to do something you really don't want to do, you gain an hour back to do something you *want* to do (like spending time with your kids or working out).

So many times, we get stuck in the rhythm of doing what we've always done, even if we don't want to do it anymore. I want you to stop and ask yourself if what you're doing is serving you.

Is there a way you can get everything accomplished without all the current stress?

7

WHY DO YOU KEEP HAVING BABIES?

TERESA'S PROBLEM

Insanity is defined as doing the same thing over and over but expecting a different outcome. Is this you?

I was on the phone with Teresa, who was complaining about how bad her life was.[6] "I don't have enough money. I need help figuring out how to invest," she said.

"Okay, I can show you how to invest," I said. "But investing takes money. You can't just show up and pull money out of thin air."

---

6 This is a real story. I've changed the name to protect her privacy.

"Well, I don't really have money right now," she said.

When I asked her why, she told me she has three kids.

I understand that. Being a single mom with three kids is hard. I asked her if there was a way she could save more money, because as a single mom with three kids, she didn't have time to go out and *make* more money. I asked her, "How can you save more. Can you squeeze some bills that you currently have? Can you get a roommate who also has kids?"

When we started going over it, she said, "I could get a roommate, and I could be the one who stays home with the kids. Because I'm pregnant again."

My response: "Holy. Fuck. Are you kidding me?"

I told her that this was a problem. I said, "The reason I think this is a problem is because you are about to bring another child into a world where you can't even afford to take care of the three you already have." I asked her what made it okay in her mind for her to continue to have sex. And I had to break it down even further, because most people don't think about babies when they think of having sex. I have yet to figure out why people don't connect sex with babies.

Teresa had not connected the idea of sex and babies, so I asked her, "Why do you keep doing baby-making activities when you know you can't afford to have any more babies?" That question helped her make the connection.

At that point, I was invested in helping her, so I started digging in more. I asked her if she can start splitting the bills with the new father—because it takes two to make a baby—and she told me that he won't be around because they broke up. Digging further, I found that she broke up with him; she didn't like how things were going. I'm now thinking, *Fuck, this is depressing.* She was in a financial situation where she couldn't afford her current kids, decided to have another child with someone else, and then kicked that man to the curb once she was pregnant. Even if he was a bum, at least he could have stayed home to watch the kids. Instead, she made it that much harder on herself to be able to invest, level up, and even simply take care of the three current kids she had.

This is a true story, and while I want to say I feel sorry for her, I don't. She put herself in that situation, just as many others do. People put themselves in these predicaments and create stressful situations for themselves. It's an unfortunate reality, one that doesn't need to happen. Stop engaging in baby-making behaviors so you stop having babies, because they are costing you a lot of money.

BABIES ARE SLOWING YOUR FINANCIAL GROWTH

In the previous chapter, we learned that having a kid will cost a middle-income married couple $284,570 over eighteen years. I bet that number came as a shock to you. That's because most people haven't assigned a dollar amount to each kid. People keep having kids because they haven't literally sat down and asked, "What is this next kid going to cost me?" Instead, they just keep popping them out.

If you invested that money instead, you'd have a much better financial future. The chart below shows how much money you could invest if you start having babies at twenty-five on the left versus how much money you can invest if you wait to have babies at thirty-five on the right.

Imagine doing this, times two or three kids.

$15,000 A YEAR INVESTED AT A 10 PERCENT RETURN (CONSERVATIVE)	
Year 1	$16,500 ($15,000 + $1,500 at 10 percent return)
Year 2	$33,150 ($16,500 + $1,650 at 10 percent return + another $15,000 that you would've needed for child)
Year 3	$51,465 ($33,150 + $3,315 at 10 percent return + another $15,000 that you would've needed for child)
Year 4	$71,611 ($51,465 + $5,146 at 10 percent return + another $15,000 that you would've needed for child)
Year 5	$93,772 ($71,611 + $7,161 at 10 percent return + another $15,000 that you would've needed for child)
Year10	$242,597
Year 18	Just under $1.1 million

So, in the next eighteen years, do you want an "Oops, I didn't mean to get pregnant" adult child, *or* do you want a million dollars? There's no wrong answer here, but you have to deal with the consequences of your choice.

WHY DO WE HAVE SO MANY BABIES?

So, why does this keep on happening? I can think of a couple of reasons...

Reason #1: Avoid Accountability

There are a couple of reasons why people keep having babies—and almost none of them are good ones. One is a lack of accountability. When some people have kids, they have stupid reasons why.

"Oh, I just can't help it."

"Oh, I'm allergic to condoms."

"Oh, my boyfriend is irresponsible. He didn't pull out."

No. You didn't do everything you needed to do to not have kids. It's not the condom's fault. It's not the boyfriend's fault. *You* have to take responsibility and be accountable for yourself. You have to ask yourself, "Did I do everything in my power to not have kids?" If your boyfriend keeps acting irresponsibly, then maybe you need to stop having sex.

Reason #2: False Sense of Confidence

Another reason is that people aren't self-aware enough. For instance, think of someone who is overweight. They have diabetes, and the doctor has literally told them, "You are in this situation because of what you are eating. If you don't change, you will die." Then, that person goes right back into the kitchen and eats the same unhealthy crap. There's a feeling people get from doing the same thing over and over again, whether that's having sex or eating the shit that gave you diabetes. For many people, that feeling is worth the risk that comes from doing the same activity repeatedly. Smokers know that cigarettes are not good for them and will give them lung cancer. However, when they do it one more time, and they don't get an adverse reaction, they're going to do it again. "The last time I smoked, my lungs didn't hurt, so I can do it again."

The same situation happens with sex. Single mothers go through a process of saying, "Fuck it. No more. I'm done with sex." Then, they have a bad day, a little slip, and have sex again. But if they don't get pregnant the time they slip up, it tells their brain, "Well, shit. We got away with it. We can get away with it one more time." Every time they don't get pregnant, it further confirms they can get away with having sex. This happens with sex, food, smoking, and drinking. Every time we do something we know we're not supposed to be doing and get away with it, the impulse grows to do it again. This is called a false sense of confidence, and it can ruin your life.

I see this all the time in the stock market. As part of my day-trading program, I tell people to trade stocks in a specific way. I'll tell them, "You're going to buy this and keep it for six months. Not a day less than six months." I always get a person who says, "I heard you, but I'm going to try it out for a week." So they buy that stock, hold it for a week, and make some money. That makes them think, *Oh, I'm the exception. I can get away with this shit.* So instead of doing it for six months like I told them, they'll keep buying stock for a week at a time. Without fail, they end up losing money because of their false sense of confidence.

You can have sex a hundred times, but it only takes one time to get pregnant. Then, you have to come up with $15,809 a year, per kid.

DON'T CHOOSE INSTANT GRATIFICATION OVER DELAYED CONSEQUENCES

This comes back to instant gratification and its evil twin: delayed consequences. If you don't have an instant negative response, you'll keep playing the game. For example, if I touch a stove, it's going to burn the shit out of me, and I'll never touch it again. But if I touch it and it doesn't burn me, I'll keep touching it. Three weeks later, I get a big-ass boil on my hand that now hurts like hell, because I took for granted the stove would be cool to touch, not burning hot. It's instant gratification versus delayed consequences.

The key message here is that you need to pay more attention to what brings you instant gratification and what has a delayed consequence.

When it comes to instant gratification, you need to think about the entire journey of an action, not just the start. The start feels great, sure, but what's the final result? For example, if I need money really badly, and I go out and rob a bank, sure, the start of that action is that I get money now. However, the journey of that action is not so good. The journey starts with getting money, but now people are looking for me because the money I took wasn't mine. What happens from there? I'm going to get killed or locked up by the people who are looking for me.

With instant gratification, we don't look at the roadmap. We just see the thing we're trying to get. So with sex, we say, "Hey, I'm going to have sex because I'm horny as hell." But when you look at the journey, you see that sex leads to babies, which leads to increased financial strain.

There are a few reasons we don't look at instant gratification as a journey. For one, we live in a microwave society. By that, I mean we want something fast (cook my meal in two minutes instead of taking thirty minutes in the oven), but I also mean that we don't think of the consequences that microwave is going to bring us in the future (radiation, potential cancer, etc.). Secondly, we have created words to block us from how things really are. So, when someone says, "Hey, I'm going to put this in the microwave and cook your food," that sounds sweet, doesn't it? "I'm going to cook your food." How sweet. However, when you say what you're really doing, it changes what you think about the action. If someone puts your food in the microwave, they should say, "Hey, I'm going to go nuke your food." That doesn't sound quite so sweet, does it? It makes you feel like they're filling it with radiation (which they are).

Consider another example. When someone puts eggs and bacon on a plate for breakfast, it sounds sweet because you remember your mom putting eggs and bacon on a plate for you. But what we should be saying is, "Okay, we have scrambled chicken fetuses and cooked stomach lining of a pig on a plate." If we said it that way, not many people would eat it.

We've changed the way we talk about things in order to desensitize ourselves to what's actually happening and avoid thinking about the action and the consequences. It may not even be a consequence for the person themself. Let's say three-year-old Lisa's parents told her, "Hey, this food on your plate, we killed it this morning. It's that little animal you were petting and that you loved so much." Well, three-year-old Lisa is now going to become a vegan very early on because she didn't want them to kill that animal for her breakfast. The fact that Lisa was never desensitized to it means she can never forget that what she's about to eat is essentially death.

A lot of us in society have had words put into place so we are desensitized from what the action is and, ultimately, desensitized from the consequences. The way we speak of things makes them sound better than what they actually are. By calling a studio apartment cozy, it makes it feel inviting, instead of calling it small and cramped. These phrases are little white lies that make us feel better. Instead of saying, "I'm going to have sex," say, "I'm going to engage in baby-making actions."

Sex brings a lot of instant gratification and a lot of delayed consequences. Pregnancy is just one example. Sometimes the consequence is your health. Many STDs can affect your health for years, if not the rest of your life. Suppose you're being careless because you want to feel good at the moment. In that case, you're trading instant gratification for a delayed consequence like HIV, which can be a life-ending event.

HOW INSTANT GRATIFICATION AFFECTS YOUR HEALTH

You work against yourself when you don't take care of your health.

For men, the more we ejaculate, the worse it is for us. It's actually the equivalent of running a marathon. When you run a marathon, you have to do a lot of stuff to recover, including getting the proper nutrition and hydration. You rarely see people run two or three marathons a week. But when it comes to sex, we run those marathons, and we never do the recovery. A lot of men get prostate cancer or prostate enlargement because they ejaculate too much (and consume too much sugar and alcohol, which dries it out). Every time you ejaculate, it enlarges the prostate, and if you don't do anything to help shrink the prostate afterward, it will keeps enlarging, which can start creating issues.

I know some of you don't believe the marathon comparison, but think about what you are really doing when you are having sex. You are engaging in an activity to *make a human being,* which means a man has to kick out enough nutrients to create that human. He's literally giving up a piece of himself to make another one of him. Believe the marathon comparison now?

Sex can affect your mental health as well. When we do things we like, we focus on them a lot. If I'm having a lot of sex, it's because I like doing that, and if I like doing that, it's taking up real estate in my mind. So instead of me focusing on my business and trying to get to F-U Money—doing what I need to do to be a better person—I'm focusing on having sex tonight. What positions are we going to do? How are we going to go down? What's the foreplay going to be? Mentally, it takes away from what I should be focusing on.

It's also mentally depressing. If you are hyping yourself up all day for sex, and then it doesn't happen the way you intended (or at all), it's depressing and stressful. Women know this very well because there are a lot of unhealthy men out there. If you're with a man and you're gonna have sex, and you think, yes, I've been waiting for this all day or all month, and then that man ejaculates within a few minutes, you're pissed. You've been anticipating and building this event up, and it was trash. Now you're mad at him, *and* you're mad at yourself for putting in the energy to get to this point.

When you are frustrated and feel a lack of appreciation, it creates an emotional craving. When you're mad at someone, you feel salty, so you crave salt. Then you start eating salty foods like fries and potato chips, which pushes you further down the unproductive ladder.

This goes back to the journey of our actions. You're having a lot of sex but having a lot of letdowns, which is making you mad. When you get mad, you emotionally make poor food choices. These poor food choices slow you down, causing you to be less productive. If you aren't productive, you aren't making as much money. If you aren't making enough money, you can't invest, and you get stuck in a paycheck-to-paycheck situation. And it all started with sex.

You don't have to fully stop having sex, but you need to have better sex management. When you get better with sex management, you are able to get more focused. For example, my friend Kay is one of the most successful people I know.[7] She also happens to be a virgin. At thirty-seven, she's never had sex. But she made $50 million in 2021 alone. Nothing takes her mind off her focus. I've tried to hook Kay up with friends, but she's so focused that she doesn't even realize when people are flirting with her.

Now, this is an extreme example, but it illustrates how this works. If you start to hold back on sex, or even become more disciplined with it, you start to get more focused. Don't get me wrong; I am a hornball for my lady. But there are times when I need to focus, and I have to tell her, "Hey, I'm not icing you out, but it's gonna be less frequent this month," so I can stay more focused.

---

7 Name changed to protect her privacy.

TIPS FROM TAY

Think about cheating. It's the ultimate instant gratification. A piece of meat walks by, be it man or woman, and you think, "My God, I'd love to sample that." So you spend time trying to make this thing happen, and in less than an hour, the instant gratification of that sample is over, and for what? Now, if you're married or in a committed relationship, you're at risk of losing everything. For what? One experience of instant gratification that took you less than an hour to do. This is why I tell men that women will fuck your shit up (and women, the same applies to you—men will fuck your shit up). If you don't get that sex component under control, it'll hurt your shit for the rest of your life.

If sex becomes your priority, you'll put everything behind it. Our actions will say, "Fuck my family; fuck my spouse. They can have the house and kids. I want this sex right now." And that can completely destroy your life.

Getting my sex urges under control is the number one thing that helped me to level up. By not having a girlfriend and not chasing ass, sex didn't control me. Instead, I focused on my money.

Instant gratification can also affect your time. When you avoid instant gratification, you can control your time and increase your discipline. I started valuing the time it takes to choose the healthier option. Instead of choosing instant gratification to get something quick, I took more time to get a more quality product or result.

For this chapter, I want you to ask yourself the following questions and write down your answers:

What is bringing you instant gratification?

_____

_____

_____

What are the possible delayed consequences to those things?

_____

_____

_____

What can you gain by avoiding instant gratification?

_____

_____

_____

8

SETTING YOUR F-U MONEY GPS

GETTING LOST

Mind your business.

Men don't like to ask for directions. We'll just keep driving.

One day, I was in Atlanta driving around. I visit Atlanta frequently, so I obviously know where I'm going, right? Ha.

Two wrong exits in a row had led me to a whole other part of the city. At this point, I didn't know where I was. Something told me, "Hey, pull over. See where you are. Then, see where you came from. Should it have taken this long?" I looked up the place where I was going and realized that it should have taken me no more than thirty minutes to get there. For reference, I'm easily an hour and a half into the drive. I told myself, "I don't know where the hell I am. Let's put it into the GPS and use directions to get where I'm trying to go. Just take the pride out of it."

I thought I knew what I was doing, but because I didn't use my GPS, the drive ended up taking three times as long as it should have. I wasted time. And in the end, I *still* ended up having to use my GPS. I should have just used it at the beginning.

So many people don't set their financial GPS. They don't pay attention to their money. I love the saying "mind your business." Normally that means "leave me alone" or "don't worry about what I have going on." When I say it, I mean *literally* mind your business. Pay attention to your business, your money, your finances, and your goals.

So many people don't pay attention to their goals or where they're trying to go. If you asked the average person, "How much is in your bank account right now?" They wouldn't know because they don't check it every day. Now, I get it. Most people don't like what's in there, and they'd rather not see it. But it's important to put your face in the piss. Gross, I know, but hear me out. When a dog pisses on the carpet, you take the dog and put his face in the piss so he knows he did wrong. The more you do that to the dog, the more he understands he has to stop doing that because he doesn't want his face in the piss.

It's the same thing with humans. The more you put your face in a part of yourself you don't like, the more you'll want to change it. Let's take weight loss for example. If you're fat and you feel unsexy, then you need to lean into that. This is you. Every day, get naked and look at yourself in the mirror. Take pictures if you need to. Doing so will affect your brain enough that if you really don't like it, you'll change it. It'll force you to change your bullshit. You choose not to look at your bank account and choose not to set a GPS because you'll have to focus on how low you are in life and how far you have to go. A lot of people don't want to think about how far away their dreams are. For some people, they're really far. So instead, you don't take on responsibility and accountability.

WHY YOU NEED TO SET YOUR GPS

No matter what your F-U Money goal is, you need an investment vehicle. I'm using the word "vehicle" for a reason. A vehicle will take you to your personal promised land. However, for the vehicle to get you there, you need to know where to go. If you get in the car and don't have your GPS set, you'll just drive around for hours.

The same principle applies to your investing journey. If you don't know what F-U Money looks like for you or don't have a goal, then you'll keep working, investing, and *hustling*, with no end in sight. You won't know if you are even headed in the right direction.

When you are hustling and have your head down, you have things flowing in and out. But if you're not paying attention and setting a GPS, you'll look up and see that everything that flowed in also flowed out. There was no game plan. There was no intention. You'll look up and wonder, *Where the fuck did my check go? How am still living paycheck to paycheck after working so hard?* It's because you don't have a game plan or a budget or allocation. How is your money being allocated? What are you allocating for savings? What are you allocating for investments? What are you allocating for living expenses? While you're just grinding away, you have to stay somewhere, and because you don't have a game plan, you stay in the first place you like. You need a car, but without a game plan or a budget, you get the first car that you want, whether you can afford it or not.

By setting your GPS, you'll know what your journey will look like as you reach milestones and get close to reaching your F-U goal.

SETTING YOUR F-U GPS

Whenever I drive somewhere new, I use my GPS to get me there. Hell, I even use it to drive to familiar places because my GPS (almost) always knows what's going on with traffic and road closures. It will redirect me to a shorter, quicker, or more accessible route, so I get to my destination efficiently. Without my GPS, I would waste countless hours in traffic. That's a lot of time I could spend making money.

As you begin setting your F-U GPS, think about these questions:

1. What does your life look like when you reach your F-U Money goal?

2. Who are the people around you, either in your circle or as your neighbors, when you get to your goal? This can be *anyone*: Is there a celebrity you want to sit at a table with? Do you want to live next door to your favorite artist or sports star?

3. What are you doing as a hobby when you reach F-U Money? Do you want to skydive? Learn how to fly a plane?

To help illustrate this, let me tell you how I answered these questions.

How My Life Looks

A lot of people are impressed with where I am, and they want to know what makes me keep going. It's true I could just live life and hang out, but I know I have a lot more to go.

When I was starting out, I set my GPS, and I accomplished everything I put on my route. The first time I started mapping out my destination, I didn't know how I was going to get there. I didn't know how I was going to make the money. I just knew that there were a few milestones that I was going to pass on my route, so here's I wrote down:

- I will move to Puerto Rico in eight years.

- I will be making $25,000 a month.

- I will be married within the next eight years.

- I will help one thousand people with their health.

I would write these goals down every day to remind me why I was waking up so early (*Oh, because I have these goals.*). When I had a little extra money, I would write them down to remind myself why I wasn't going out and spending the money. Writing these goals reminded me where I was going and why I was sacrificing.

I ended up hitting all of those goals (except Puerto Rico) well before my eight-year deadline. In fact, I hit them in just two years. It was time to rinse and repeat. I wasn't about to stop at $25,000 a month. I was not about to stop at a thousand new clients. Instead, I set a new GPS, and I wrote down new goals:

- I will make $100,000 a month.

- I will help five thousand people with their health.

- I will be living in Puerto Rico.

- I will acquire real estate.

Within four years, all of those goals came to fruition. In fact, while my goal was to help five thousand people, I ended up helping fifteen thousand. Once I hit those goals, I set new ones that I'm still working toward. Now, instead of writing down my goals, I've started to visualize my goals instead. (Don't worry; we'll get to that in a minute.)

The People around Me

When I was starting out, I knew that the majority of the people I had around me were no good for where I was trying to go. These were people who had "stinkin' thinkin'." They were negative. Everything that I tried to do to better myself, they had something negative to say about it. When I invested in a coach, they would say, "Why would you give somebody a thousand dollars? That's stupid. You can google everything you need to know." (Not true, by the way.) When I went vegan and wanted to work more on my health, they would say, "Why are you eating like that? You're eating like a white person." Hand to God, people would say shit like that to me. "Give me your Black card. You're not Black anymore because you eat like that." I have a smart mouth (shocking, I know), so I would usually answer back with something like "So what you're telling me is that eating healthy is eating like a white person. So, what do you eat? It sounds like you eat like shit. When you eat like shit, it comes with diabetes and high blood pressure. Know what happens when you have those? Your dick doesn't work."

Having these kinds of conversations made me resentful and allowed me to push people away. I knew they were bad for me, so I went into this loner place where I didn't want anybody around. You have to tear down before you rebuild, so I tore down everybody around me. As I stayed in that space of betterment, reading books and going to seminars, I started meeting other people who were also loners. We started to lock arms and pretty soon, I had whole new surroundings. Not because I actively went out and searched for them. We found each other because we wanted the same things.

I tell people, "Show me the five people you're hanging around, and I'll show you your future." When you say something like that, it makes people think, *Oh, I better go find better friends.* No. Don't get rid of the friends. Work on *yourself*. If these friends are meant to be around, they'll grow with you. If they're not, they'll leave on their own, and a new circle of friends will find you because you're going to be in the same place: at the same restaurants, at the same gym, at the same seminars.

My Evolving Hobby

At first, one of my favorite hobbies was to play basketball. Back then, I wanted to create more time so that I could play ball with no worries. I didn't want to have to worry about bills or what was going on with my job; I just wanted to go play ball and be free.

Then it started to evolve because as your finances evolve, so do your hobbies. I went from playing to watching—I still play occasionally, but let's be real; I'm getting older and my knees don't enjoy playing as much as I do. I love going to NBA games. In fact,

I love the game so much that I don't even have a favorite team. (I do have a few favorite players though.) If the teams are good, I will go to any game and cheer for any team because I just like the sport.

As my finances evolved, so did my experience of the game. Now I can get floor seats, which is a completely different experience from watching in the stands. There are different entries and exits for people on the floor. You don't have to walk up to the concession stand to go get food. Instead, there's a whole cafe downstairs with food that's laid out and *free*. You just go in, grab food, grab something from the open bar, and dig in. That experience is a completely different level of hobby. You get to meet a bunch of fun people, you get to network, and you get to sit at arm's length from legendary players.

VISUALIZE WHAT YOU WANT

Everyone has a big-ticket item they have wanted since they were a kid. I'm not talking about a fancy new phone—I'm talking about major, life-changing purchases you can't make when you are scraping by.

What is it that you want? It could be a mansion, a yacht, a trip to space (we're doing that now, apparently), or a fucking gold toilet seat. Once you know what it is you want, you need to visualize it in order to manifest it into your life. (Don't roll your eyes at this "woo-woo" talk. It works. If it worked for Oprah and Will Smith, it'll work for you. Just have a little trust, okay?)

There are two ways to do visualizations. The first way, which is the most popular, is to get a picture of what it is you want and put it everywhere. Print one out and tape it to your fridge, make it the background on your phone and laptop, or whatever—just make sure it's somewhere visible.

The second way is my preferred way because you can hold your dream. Go on Amazon or Etsy and buy a small model of what it is you want, and put it somewhere you can see, daily. Hell, if you want to, you can cuddle it at night. This is a physical manifestation of your vision.

I used the model manifestation method with all three of my cars—though I didn't know it at the time. Three years ago, I bought three miniature cars: a blue Lamborghini, a black Mercedes truck, and a black McLaren. I kept them on a shelf in my office. Even once I was "rich," I didn't buy them. Instead, I kept reinvesting. Until, finally, I realized that my GPS was set to these cars—but I had driven right past my marker. So I went out and bought the black McLaren first. Then, I bought my black Mercedes truck. Lastly, I decided to buy my Lamborghini. I told my broker to find me a black Aventador Lamborghini, but he said there wasn't one in the entire country. The only one he could find was baby blue; I decided to buy it anyway. A few days later, when I was looking back through my old videos (I had lost my models during my divorce), I realized that I had purchased the exact make and color cars that I had once had models of on the shelf. My Lamborghini is the exact same shade of blue as my model. Without realizing it, I manifested exactly what I wanted.

For me right now, it's a jet. Since I was nineteen years old, I have wanted my own personal jet. So I went out and bought a small model jet, put it together, and put it on my bedside table. I look at it every day and visualize the day I will have my own.

YOUR GPS MUST INCLUDE THE THREE TENETS OF SUCCESS

The definition of success relies on three tenets.

1. Having healthy relationships with spouses, family, friends, and business partners.

2. Being physically healthy.

3. Being financially healthy.

Healthy versus Toxic Relationships

Now, I am not a therapist. However, from my experience, a healthy experience is a loving, supporting, and serving relationship. Each person should be there to serve each other. If your back hurts, I'll give it a massage. If it's itching, I'll scratch it. We are here to love each other, support each other, and help each other. It's not just teamwork; it's a team. It should be one relationship, not just two separate people coming together. It's two people that are now one on the same journey with the same mindset who want the same things. You should be compatible.

In a toxic relationship, there's competition in the household, where one person wants to outdo the other. In a competition, there's technically no rules. It's just about winning and beating the other person. When you start competing with your person, you do whatever you can to win. Sometimes that is outdoing the other person, and sometimes it's pulling the other person down. That's a very toxic relationship because at that point, no one wins. In a healthy relationship, no one wins because my wins are supposed to be your wins. In a toxic relationship, because you are trying to compete with me, you're actively trying to dial me back. You see my wins as your losses. That's toxic, unsupportive, and unloving. People who love you won't do shit like that.

Physically Healthy versus Unhealthy

Being physically healthy means having active daily movement and active daily nourishment. A lot of times, it's not necessarily your physical look that says you're healthy. I've seen people at 5 percent body fat who are trash internally.

Health is an active daily thing. Are you eating the things your body needs to perform? Are you getting enough water? Are you eating the right nutrients? I've been unhealthy in my nutrients before. In my attempt to get leaner, I cut out vegetables in order to cut down on carbs. But I finally realized how unhealthy it is to cut out vegetables and wondered what the fuck I was doing. You have to be careful with nutrients because it can be a thin line. Overall, you need to eat right and make sure you are getting the right food groups, nutrients, and vitamins. Some people do green powders (I love my green powders). Once you get your eating habits down, you need to commit to daily physical activity as well.

I suggest a minimum of three workout sessions a week to remain active. However, we need to move at least a little bit daily because we need to increase our blood flow on a day-to-day basis. Why? Because we have something called a stroke volume. This is where the blood circulates throughout the body, and what happens is that it moves things around, including any toxicity and nutrients. First off, we want to move nutrients to our brains so they work better. But on the flip side, if you don't move that water, it breeds bacteria. Think about it: your body is 80 percent water. You have all of this water in your body, and if you're not moving it around, then it's sitting, collecting bacteria. And stagnant bacteria is no bueno.

Financially Healthy versus Unhealthy

We can simplify all three of these sections to ask: are you loving the thing we're talking about? In a relationship, are you being loving? In health, are you loving your body? The same thing goes for money. Are you loving your money? Are you doing right by your money? Are you budgeting, allocating for savings, saving for retirement? To be financially healthy is to be financially in charge. You know what's going on; you are actively working inside your finances. You need to be a good shepherd of your money.

For me, being financially healthy is being in control of and taking care of your money.

While being financially healthy can look different based on the person, just like being physically healthy can look different to a range of people, there is a general sense of financial health. This includes things like making your money work for you, outpacing inflation each year, and being in a position to handle emergencies that may come up.

For example, I have a student that I worked with who utilized some of the principles I taught her in my program, Secure The Bag. Every time she spent money on something she didn't need, she put the equivalent amount in a brokerage account to invest. One of these items was her luxury car (a brand-new Lexus). She didn't need a car with a $400 a month payment, so she not only paid $400 a month for the car but also put $400 a month into a brokerage account. This let her grow her money in her sleep, outpace inflation, and have spare money for emergencies—all because she worked on her financial fitness.

BEING SUCCESSFUL

To be successful, you must have all three. Not just one or two— *all three*. If you have great relationships and a lot of money, but you are unhealthy, you won't be able to enjoy them for long. When you set your GPS, you need to know what you want your life to look like in each of these three areas. You need to spend time working on each one because you can't have a full, rewarding life without them. If you neglect your friends or marriage, you'll be lonely no matter how in shape you are or how much money you have. It's all about a healthy balance.

Once you have all three, you can set your GPS. If you try to set your GPS before you have these things, you'll make your journey harder and create more work for yourself. "Okay, I set my GPS...but my shit is in chaos." It's the same as setting the GPS in your car. Great, good for you; you set the GPS. But you don't have gas, you didn't change the oil, and you have a flat tire because you didn't take care of the car. So now you're ready to go, except you're *not* ready to go because you can't go anywhere with your car busted.

TIPS FROM TAY

I have three ways to keep my relationships, health, and finances on point.

1. Relationships: I work to keep communication clear and schedule quality time with those I love and have close relationships with, such as my wife, family, and close friends.

2. Health: I make sure to dedicate *at least* one hour to my health each day, such as showering and brushing my teeth. I don't do a single thing until I have cared for my hygiene and health for the day.

3. Financial: One of my daily practices is my Money Minute. This is where I quickly check all my financial accounts and make plans to get to the next level based on the condition of those accounts. I grew up poor and never want to go back, so financial health is critical for me.

How do you keep your relationships, health, and finances in check and on track?

PART TWO

OUR F-U VEHICLES

At this point, you should know why you need to get your life in order, how to get your life in order, and how to set your F-U GPS. Now, we're going to learn how to earn our F-U Money. The majority of wealthy people got wealthy in one of four ways: entrepreneurship (owning a business of some kind), playing the stock market, buying crypto, or investing in real estate. However, the first thing you need to do to get to any of the other vehicles is to build a business through entrepreneurship.

When I talk about entrepreneurship (which we'll dive into more in the next chapter), I mean building a business that doesn't require you to work 100 percent of the time to earn money. It should make you money while you eat. It should make you money while you sleep. It should make you money while you are on vacation.

Once you make money through your business, you can begin to drive other vehicles. Take the stock market, for instance. To play the market correctly, you need money. But not nearly as much money as you do to begin investing in real estate. Once you are in the stock market, you can start looking into crypto. However, know that crypto is a much more speculative market. With the stock market, we have hundreds of years of data to work with. Crypto has only been around for about fifteen. I don't think it's wise to put more than 20 percent of your net worth into crypto.

As you move through these chapters, you'll notice the vehicles become either riskier or more cost-intensive. That's why we are leaving crypto and real estate for last—crypto is a little like "buying air," and getting started in real estate takes a lot of capital.

Now, risk is relative, and the amount of risk depends on the parameters around it. In my opinion, crypto is the riskiest because it doesn't have a history behind it. But really, all of these are risky if you jump in not knowing what you are doing. You can buy a piece of real estate, and it will not turn over any profits if you don't know how to get a tenant or how to find people to rehab it.

So where should you start?

- If you have more time than money, you should start with entrepreneurship.

- If you have more money than time, you should start with the stock market.

- If you are already making a lot of money from the stock market, you should start with crypto.

- If you can invest in the stock market and crypto and still have disposable income, then you can *consider* starting in real estate.

Once you know which vehicle to start with, you need to review your GPS. Does your overall life vision include you working a lot, for example? If not, then entrepreneurship likely isn't the end path for you. It may be a good starting path, but you should aim to work your way off of that path and into the stock market, crypto, and real estate, all vehicles that require more money but less work.

How you divide up your money into these four vehicles will depend on how you have set your GPS. What does your F-U Money journey look like when you get there? If you want to travel the world and not have to work—you just want money coming in no matter what you do—then dividend-paying stock is going to be your best bet. You'll need to figure out how much money you need, then you can figure out which stock to invest in.

As you read these chapters, keep your GPS in mind. Think about how each investment vehicle fits (or doesn't) in your journey. If you want your money to work for you, you don't want to go into entrepreneurship. Instead, you should think about going into stocks. However, even then, you need to narrow down how you want to invest in stocks. If you want passive money, you should look into dividends instead of growth stock. Over the last five to ten years, 70 percent of the profits that were taken out of the stock market came from dividends.

9

ENTREPRENEURSHIP

INFLUENCES ON MY ENTREPRENEURIAL JOURNEY

You'll never get rich trading hours for dollars.

People always think there's a beautiful story behind any successful entrepreneur, or that there was an influential and positive person behind him. No. For me, the influences who had a big impact on my entrepreneurial journey were drug dealers. Drug dealers had everything I wanted. They had time because they didn't have to work a lot. If they had a dime bag of weed that was $10, and they needed $1,000 a week, they just needed ten people a day to buy a bag. If you only need ten people a day and you only have to spend five minutes with each person, that's only an hour a day on work—everything else is your free time. Of course, you had the people who took it to the next level. They got a little bigger, started selling bigger things, and started having employees who helped them sell.

These were all entrepreneurs. They were literally using supply and demand. They had a big impact on me because I saw how the system worked, and I knew that you could plug any product into this system. So yeah, drug dealers were influences on me. These guys may have been rough around the edges, but they had time, they got women, they had nice cars (because they could make money quick), and they had nice clothes. While I was spending eight hours a day working, they were hanging out because they had already made their money for the day.

Not only did I see this happen up close in my neighborhood, but I saw it in movies. *Scarface* is one of my favorite movies, as is *Paid in Full*. These movies influenced me as well because these characters started a business, sold a product that had a high demand, and then took the money they made from their high-demand product and put it back into their business. That is a great business model. Unfortunately, they were selling something that wasn't legal.

MY ENTREPRENEURSHIP ROOTS

My grassroots are in entrepreneurship. Everything I have came from my business. I had no money, but I had time and a willingness to work. I started off working at a warehouse to make enough money to get certified as a trainer. Once I got my certification, I was able to start training people.

The catch? I started off working for free.

You read that right. The first three months as a certified personal trainer, I offered my training services for free. I didn't charge a single cent. At that time, my only goal was to get experience and get better.

Instead of charging, I kept my job at the warehouse so I could pay my bills. During my breaks, I would read constantly. One of my coworkers, Randy, noticed me and asked why I read so much. I told him my dream of being a full-time personal trainer and my goal of personal improvement. (At the time, I was working toward a certification in nutrition.) Randy told me, "Hey, I have a personal trainer who owns a boutique gym. I think you should meet him." Randy set up an introduction, and I met the owner of Impact Fitness, Ben, at 4:00 a.m. (he wanted to meet before he started working with his clients for the day). The meeting went great, and Ben was impressed with my ambition and drive. He invited me to start hanging around at the gym to get some clients.

It was at this point I realized that *this* was what I was supposed to do. So I quit my job—I literally walked out the door with no backup plan. I went to Impact and hung around for ten to twelve hours a day. I swept and mopped floors for free in an attempt to get paying clients.

About three months in, I got my first one. And I *smashed* it. I rocked her world. The biggest thing I did had nothing to do with technical results. When she first started as a client, she had reservations about personal trainers, and she was worried I could potentially hurt her by making her lift too much weight (she was an older lady). I rocked her world by getting her one of the best workouts she ever had by either sitting down or laying down. I did not stand her up one time. We did deep bridges, donkey kicks, planks, static holds, and other exercises like that. She burned six hundred calories in that hour by laying down. She got up and said, "That was the best workout I've ever had. I could see myself doing that well into my eighties and nineties. That's a workout that can be done forever." I knew then that I had something special because no matter who you were or what situation you were in, I could get you a good workout. As time went on, I was able to continue giving her killer workouts without the worry of her getting hurt. While we were working out, we started having conversations about the stock market and what's going on in the world, and we got to the point where she told me she considered me a really good friend. I knew then that I had a client for life.

She loved our workouts so much that she brought me three more clients. At that point, I was making about $3,000 a month, which meant I was breaking even compared to what I was making at my last job. I talked with Ben, who was impressed with my work and offered me a partnership. He asked me to be the manager of the gym for the duration of its existence, which had a seven-year lease. I knew this opportunity would give me seven years to build myself up and get the hell out of that gym.

This is when I started to build my online presence. I created YouTube and Instagram accounts, but I didn't sell anything on either platform. Instead, I created content, content, and more content—I created a presence and made my name known.

The second year, which was also the first year I hit six figures, I started my first online program. I realized then that I had a model that could work. I had gone from making $50,000 as a full-time trainer (most of that toward the end of the year) to over $100,000 in my second year. The third year went even better. I started bringing in more online clients, and I hired an online coach who taught me how to run ads on Instagram and Facebook. I went from $100,000 in my second year to $250,000 my third.

I knew it was time to start letting go of my in-person clients because I started trading time for money. Using the time I *would* have spent with those clients, I started building my online presence instead, which brought in money even while I slept. By year four, I was making $400,000 a year and realized I was making much more than I needed to live, but I didn't know what I should be doing with my extra money. I wanted to spend it on cars and jewelry, but I knew that wasn't the smart move. Instead, I hired someone who was killing it in the stock market and paid him to teach me everything he knew.

We're now in year five. I'm doing my online business full time, and I'm taking parts of my profits and investing them into the stock market. In fact, a lot of businesses will invest in their competition. I know this sounds weird, but it makes sense. Take Apple and Microsoft, for example. Apple will buy stock in Microsoft. And if for some reason, Microsoft attracts some of Apple's customers, Apple says, "Great, go ahead. When Microsoft does better, we make money." Another reason to put profit into the stock market is to earn more freedom. Say your business is going well but not great. You're paying the bills; things are fine. But then you miss a week or two—now that's going to be a hard month. You're going to miss paying a bill, or someone on your team isn't going to get paid. This creates a form of desperation because now you're willing to take any and every type of customer—because you *need* the money. You don't have a reserve. Essentially, you're living paycheck to paycheck even though you have your own business, and you're stuck taking on assholes just to get by. If you invest your profits, you'll be able to take clients you want to work with. You'll have the ability to say no to working with assholes. You can take vacations. You can create this lifestyle of comfort and the ability to survive on your own terms.

Back to year five. At this point in my entrepreneurial journey, the gym owners had noticed my online presence and told me that my business was a conflict of interest, as they were going to have to start competing with it. So they let me go. This was the best thing ever. Why? Because of the $400,000 I was making a year, $350,000 of it was coming from my online business.

A MOOR MENTALITY

Getting fired lit a *fire* under my ass. It gave me a Moor mentality. When the Moors went to conquer Spain, they immediately burned their ships upon landing. They were either going to conquer or die—there was no turning back. This was the mentality I took on when I was fired. I was going to make this work. Period.

By the close of year five, all of my attention was on my online business and the stock market, and I had brought in a little over a million dollars. I was now sure this was the real deal and what I was meant to do. I had burned my ships, and there was no going back.

Years six and seven, I stayed stagnant at about a million a year. At year eight, nine, and ten, I was no longer doing personal training. I was making great money from trading stocks. I had a good amount of money in my brokerage account. I thought that I could live off my portfolio, so I retired. However, I continued to post on my social media because one of the biggest assets we have in this day and age is our digital real estate. By year ten, I had about 500,000 followers. I was no longer trying to sell anything on it, and instead, I just posted about my lifestyle. My goal was to maintain attention because I knew I could turn it back into a money-making asset any time I needed to.

As I continued posting, people started asking me how I was making so much money from the stock market. And I said, "Well, I can teach it to you." Turns out, people really want that knowledge. I gained a huge influx of followers once I started talking about the stock market. That led to me starting a new business: Secure The Bag. Secure The Bag is where I teach people how to trade on the stock market, how to read charts, how to assess a company and see if it's profitable, and how to know if you should buy or sell.

I started my prices very modestly at $50 a month. As I got more results and more clients, I started to raise prices to $200 a month, then $500 a month, then $1,000 a month, then to

$5,000 a year. This scaling method is the exact method that the drug dealers I saw used to scale their businesses.

By this point, I went from making one million dollars a year to about five million dollars a year—and then things really got crazy. I took the extra money from this new business and started day trading in the stock market. I made an *additional* six to seven figures a year from day trading.

ENTREPRENEURSHIP IS NOT FOR THE FAINT OF HEART

I won't sugarcoat this for you. *Entrepreneurship is hard.* It's hard physically and emotionally. I worked in a gym for twelve hours a day, and when I went home, I continued to work because that's what I had to do to get my business off the ground. Unlike a nine-to-five job, entrepreneurship doesn't stop when you leave. When you go home, there's still more work to do. There's still more time to put in. You have to give your body and energy to build a business. I sacrificed my twenties to build what I have now. I didn't go out and party. I wasn't chasing ass. I didn't smoke or drink. I followed all of the tenets you've read so far.

It takes an emotional toll as well. I didn't spend time with my family and friends. I didn't go see my mom or brother often. I didn't spend time with my girlfriend. I was busy working. It's draining emotionally when you realize you don't have time to spend with people *and* build your business. It's also hard because your people will make it known they are upset at your lack of time.

Mine would tell me:

"You don't call me like you used to."

"You don't take me on dates like you used to."

It's hard emotionally because I *wanted* to hang out and do all the things, but I was also dead-focused on doing better for myself and my family. It was emotionally hard for me, so it probably will be for you too.

Entrepreneurship is also mentally hard. I had a roommate for years. As much as I wanted my own space, I needed help paying bills and making ends meet. I also needed someone who could help me while I was building my business. Luckily, I was very good friends with my roommate, and he was supportive of what I was trying to do. When I was working for free, he paid my cell phone bill. He would drop me off and pick me up at the gym every day. He took care of my rent. We came to an agreement that he would give me six months to get on my feet. I told him that if he could take care of me and the bills for six months, I would pay him back. I needed help and a support system.

All too well, I know what it feels like to want your own space and be on your own. But you have to *earn* that. You have to work, and work *hard,* to afford those things. I was a grown man who was living with a roommate—I had another man taking care of me. I didn't have a car. I didn't have my own place. I couldn't afford my own cell phone. But I made it work, and now I'm at the top of my game.

Being on the top is great, but the journey to get to the top is extremely hard. You have to be tough enough to handle it.

I lived up to my promise, by the way. My former roommate and best friend is now my business partner, and we still take care of each other.

SOLOPRENEUR VERSUS ENTREPRENEUR

A solopreneur is someone who only makes money when they work. It's only them in the business, and they may make good money, but they don't really own a *business*—they own a *job*. It's hard for a solopreneur to get F-U Money because when they stop working, they stop making money.

An entrepreneur owns a business. When they step away from the business, it will continue to make money. When they go to sleep, they make money. When they go on vacation, they make money. When they spend a few weeks in the hospital, they still make money.

This distinction is very important. Many people mix these terms up and assume that being a solopreneur is the same as being an entrepreneur—it's not. If you want to make money while you sleep and while you are on vacation, passively, then you need to know that. You need to take actions and make decisions in order to create passive income instead of just looking in the mirror and saying, "I make my own money. I'm an entrepreneur!"

No.

You need to take that money and pour it back into the business. You need to set up systems that will make money for you while you are doing whatever you want to do. The goal should be passive income. That's how you get to F-U Money.

There are several ways to generate passive income. The biggest way is to generate intellectual property, by writing a book, for example. Not only does writing a book make you an authority in your space, but it also generates additional income that you can make in your sleep. Another way is to make a teaching course on something you are an expert in. You can make the videos, upload them to a system like Kajabi or Teachable, and from there, you can make $99/month per person without having to show up, because you've already done the work.

DON'T CALL YOURSELF A SMALL BUSINESS OWNER

I hate the phrase "small business owner." When you think about a small business, people assume you don't make a lot of money.

That's just not true. A small business is defined by having a small number of employees. It's a small business because it's not a big operation.

Technically, I am a small business with ten employees—and I make a lot of money. One of my friends owns a company with a thousand employees, and he's considered a big business. He brings in about $12 million a year in revenue, while I bring in $20 million. Small business does not mean small profits. When you are considered a small business, a lot of people will write you off. But you can have a small amount of personnel and still make a large amount of money.

All of this to say: get the negative connotations of a small business out of your head. Don't let the term hold you back.

HOW TO SCALE YOUR BUSINESS

Number one, when you have more time than money, you must put the time into your business. There's no way around it. You have to go hard to do this and put the time in. This is going to take more than a nine-to-five. You are going to have to work more than eight hours a day. You're going to have to skip watching TV sometimes (or all the time). You're going to have to give up some weekends. You're going to have to give up some vacations. You're going to have to make sacrifices. However, if you do make those sacrifices, you'll be able to live better than you ever dreamed of. Sacrifice now—work hard *now*—for long-term gain. It sucks, but it works. I'm living proof.

Number two, use your free resources while you have them. A big part of the work you put into your business isn't going to be client work. A lot of the time is going to be study time, trying to find out how to run a business or how to start YouTube or Instagram accounts. You'll need answers to questions like these:

- What's an LLC?

- What's an S-Corp?

- Which do I need?

- What's a CPA?

- How are my taxes going to be done?

- What's itemizing?

- What can I write off?

You'll need to know the answers to these questions when you're first starting out as an entrepreneur, especially when coming from a nine-to-five. With a day job, you get your W-2, go to H&R Block to file your taxes, and call it a day. That won't fly as an entrepreneur.

Number three, the next step in the evolution of your business will be when you don't have the time but you have the money. Now you're going to have to spend your money (which is still a resource) to better advance your business. This means hiring a coach. Say you no longer have time to run your Instagram or Facebook accounts, and you need to run ads. It's time to hire somebody to do that. Or you can hire a coach to teach you how to do it yourself instead of wasting time you don't have trying to learn it by yourself.

TIPS FROM TAY

Fair warning: most of what I'm about to tell you, I've said already. But I believe in these methods so strongly that I want to repeat them where needed. I want this shit to stick!

The slow method to entrepreneurship is to figure it out on your own. The longer you stay in the space of trying to figure out how to run a business and scale it on your own, the longer it's going to take you to reach scalability.

However, if you want to fast-track it, wait a few years until you start making money. Once you make that money, don't spend it on bullshit—take it and find someone that you can pay for consulting, someone who has already done what you are trying to do. Pay them to teach you how to scale your business. They can tell you the pitfalls to look out for and the best place to run advertising. To scale faster, you need to have someone who has already done it teach you the cheat codes. It can cut your time in half.

Figuring it out on your own can take you ten years or more. Having someone teach you can get you there in *half* the time. Essentially, it's taking one step back to take three *leaps* forward.

We come back to time versus money. You either take the time to go through and read the books and watch the videos, or you have the money to invest in yourself and pay for mentorship and coaching. My Dave Ramsey crowd isn't going to like this, but you need to learn the proper use of debt. (Dave Ramsey is a financial wellness coach that caters to the everyday person who wants to be middle class.) In my experience, a lot of poor people have a bad relationship with debt. They take out a credit card or take out a loan and go buy a car or a house (or shoes or clothes). This makes these people a slave to whoever they owe. Rich people (or people who are more money savvy) also take on debt, but they do it the right way. They take on debt and put it into a business (say for advertising or to hire coaches to teach us the cheat codes).

I did this for my first two coaches, like we talked about in Chapter 5, and as we established in Chapter 2, Robert Kiyosaki told us to use Other People's Money to get to the top.

If you want to hire a coach, don't use your own money. Find a way to borrow somebody else's. Get a loan. (I got mine from PayPal to hire my first coach.) You don't even have to have great credit to do it.

For my newly started entrepreneur readers, I want you to open one account, either with PayPal, Stripe, or Square. Just one; don't have all three of them. What you want to do is run all of your sales through that one channel. Why? All of those companies are the new banks. They use an algorithm to determine your credit worthiness based on your sales. They don't check your credit score when supplying a loan; they check your sales.

If you are making pretty good sales and are ready to scale up, they'll say something like, "Hey, you've been doing great. Looks like you're making about $5,000 a month, so we'll give you a $10,000 loan." Then what they'll do is take five percent of each sale you make to pay back your loan. This allows you to use other people's money without even using your credit.

Before moving on, ask yourself these questions:

Does this feel like something that will be helpful on your journey?

If yes, in what specific way could you see this being helpful?

How does this fit (or not fit) into your GPS?

10

THE STOCK MARKET

LEARNING THE LESSON OF COMPOUND INTEREST

The stock market is a part of the American Dream. You can't comfortably live and enjoy America if you are not participating in the stock market in some fashion.

I was twenty-two, and I had just learned about compound interest. I learned that if you put $10,000 into something that compounds $10,000 a year, and then you keep putting in $10,000 a year, it keeps compounding to the point where you'd be a millionaire within twenty years. I knew then that this was the way to make money. A lot of people think that you can work your way there, but you can't. Minimum wage—or really any wage—is not meant to be worked at for your whole life until you retire in order to get out of working. It's only a means to an end. The main goal is to do away with trading hours for dollars.

I read a story once about a man who worked as a janitor and a gas station attendant and had quietly amassed $8 million by the time he died at ninety-two. A neighbor said that if he earned $50, he invested $40 of it. He owned at least ninety-five stocks when he died.

It proves that it is possible to get to F-U Money with a small amount of money; it just takes patience. This man was investing $40 a week, which is roughly $200 a month. With only $2,400 a year, this man compounded his investments to $8 million. This is why, at the beginning of the book, I insist that you need to stop drinking, smoking, and partying. That's an extra $500 a month that you can invest. You need to get to the point that you are willing to either be patient or put in more work so you can make more money in a shorter period of time.

MY JOURNEY INTO THE STOCK MARKET

I first got into the stock market seven years ago. As we discussed in the last chapter, I was making more money than I needed to live, and I knew I didn't want that money to just sit in the bank. I decided I wanted to put it into stocks, but I didn't know where to start. So, I asked around. The most common advice I heard was to get a financial advisor.

But I have trust issues. I wasn't about to hand over a bunch of my money to a stranger and let them decide what to do with it. Plus, most financial advisors weren't in the financial position I wanted to be in. I wanted anyone I trusted with my money to be living the life I wanted to live. There's a funny joke by Warren Buffett that says, roughly, that Wall Street is the only place people drive to in a Rolls Royce to get advice from people who ride the subway. (Warren Buffett is the Michael Jordan of the stock market. He's a G.O.A.T. He's been trading stock for the last fifty years. The man has got it *figured out*. That's why he's worth $116.9 billion (at the time of writing this book).

Instead of hiring a financial advisor, I looked into what a financial advisor would do with my money. The answer? They would put it into a balanced stock portfolio, which would earn me between 5 and 12 percent a year. Being the arrogant bastard I am, I thought, *Well, if he can make 5 to 12 percent, I can do that too.* So I started really digging into the stock market and doing research on my own. I found out that most millionaires and billionaires made their money either by way of the stock market or real estate. I decided I would do both. As I mentioned, getting into real estate costs a lot of money (I'm talking a hundred million bucks to do it right), so I waited until I had the capital to do it right. I started putting money into the stock market instead.

What I didn't do was just throw my money in there willy-nilly. At the time, I had a billionaire client I was training whose name was Charlie. He had made a lot of money through his business, then grew it exponentially in the stock market. Obviously, he was doing something right, so I asked his advice, took him seriously, and continued putting my resources into both investing and learning more about investing. Seven years later, the stock market made me millions enabled me to buy my Lamborghini.

NEVER SELL YOUR ASSETS—BUT SPEND THE MONEY

Here's a big secret they don't tell you. Rich people have a saying: "When is the best time to sell assets? Never." The houses I own, the stock I own, my gold, silver, Rolex watches—all these things with value—I will never sell. Why? Because they will just keep going up in value over time. However, when I first heard this saying, I thought, *Well, if I never sell it, how do I use the money?* I started my search by googling "how to leverage my stocks to get a loan." What I found out was that the stock market is just like real estate. You can do a home equity line of credit on property that you own, and you can do it to your stocks too.

I didn't take money out of my brokerage account to buy my Lambo. Instead, I borrowed *against* my stocks. Specifically, I put a $1 million into Apple stock, and over a few years, that Apple stock doubled in price. Once it was worth $2 million, I was able to borrow against that stock to take out $1.2 million, giving me more than enough to pay the $700,000 I needed to buy my Lambo. So, instead of just being out $700,000, my money was still in the Apple stock and still earning me money.

While I'm driving around in my Lambo (looking fucking fit, I might add) and having fun, that $2 million is still working hard for me. In ten years, when that money grows to $20 million, I'll only have to pay back two percent a year, for a grand total of $200,000. Now in ten years, I'll be out $200,000, but I'll have made $20 million. What I can do then is sell back some of the stock to pay off the rest of the loan, and I'll still have a net value close to $19 million. I'll never sell my stocks though because they will just keep growing in value.

Want to know an even bigger secret? This is how rich people get out of paying taxes. There is no tax implication on a loan. If you have $10 million in a brokerage account, and you take a $3 million loan to live off of for the next few years, you don't pay any income taxes on that loan because you have to pay it back. So you can just keep kicking those taxes down the road. This works because, technically, they're not earning money; they're borrowing money.

SO MANY FUND TYPES, SO LITTLE TIME

A fund is an institution that combines a group of different assets (such as stocks or real estate) and then hedges (spreads out the risk) across multiple assets. A lot of your funds will have no more than 15 percent of allocation in one given asset. Most have twenty to fifty assets that they are juggling. A fund is looking for the highest available return—or highest return possible—with the least amount of risk. High return with low reward is the average person's goal with starting or getting into one.

Index Funds

Index funds are an investment type that require you to play the long game. They are made to balance out over time, and they have a slow growth rate. However, index funds are a good option if you want to play it safe and avoid downsides (a.k.a. losing a bunch of money in one year). Slower growth, smaller risk. Unlike mutual funds and ETFs (exchange-traded funds), index funds invest in a specific list of securities. Mutual funds and ETFs have a list that is constantly changing based on what the investment manager believes is the best option at that time.

Mutual Funds and ETFs

I'll be honest: I'm not the biggest fan of mutual funds. They have very slow (to almost nonexistent) growth. The safer you get, the less growth you get.

However, it protects you from the downside and maximizes the upside. It's a mutual fund because it's usually mutually beneficial to you and me. That means it's mutually beneficial to the person running it and to the person who is paying to be in it. It usually has ten to thirty different assets in the fund to protect the downside while aiming for maximum growth. Mutual funds are one of the oldest tricks in the book. For example: if I start a brokerage account and you say, "I want in on what you have going on," I bring you in and say, "Okay, you give me some money and I'll put it into this brokerage account I have." Then, I'll trade it amongst the stocks that I'm playing right now.

ETFs are not really that different from a traditional mutual fund. ETFs are similar to mutual funds, but you don't come into my fund, and I trade for you. An ETF is more like a stock that is the combination of a portfolio of fifteen stocks with a set price. For example, let's say I have twenty stocks that I've purchased, and my ETF has a ticker symbol of TAY. The ticker symbol of TAY right now is worth $30. Well, if those stocks that I picked to put inside my ETF start going up (or so long as more go up than down), then the price of my ticker symbol goes up from $30 to $35. If you bought into my ETF, then every share you bought will go up in value as well.

The difference between these two can be confusing, so let's use blackjack to explain the difference. Say you walk up to the blackjack table and the person playing is really good. You're like, "Holy fuck, dude. You are really good at this. I don't want to play. How about I give you some money and you do it for me since you're so good?" So he goes in, he's playing, and he's making a killing with your money. When he's done, he gives you what he made from your money, but he also takes a 10–20 percent cut. That's the mutual fund.

Now imagine you go to the blackjack table, and the same guy is playing, but there are also five other blackjack tables around with a great player at each of those tables. Which table do you want to put your money on? If the money on one table does better than the others, that money goes up in value. Now, whenever you are ready, you can sell it and say, "Hey, I bought this table at $20, it turned a crazy profit, and I cashed out at $40." That's the ETF.

In other words, a mutual fund is betting on the person (a.k.a. fund manager) and their ability to play poker (a.k.a. pick stocks). An ETF is based on the performance of the entire group of tables playing instead of a single player (a.k.a. stock portfolio). When there's more winning tables than losing tables, you win (a.k.a. make money).

Long-Term Investing in Quality Companies

A lot of the trading done in the stock market is done over the short term: a few days, a few weeks, maybe a few months. People who do long-term investments in quality companies are looking to get in early and stay for ten to thirty *years* before selling. In fact, they might never want to sell. For me, I do both. I'll do some short-term trading, take the profit, and put it into my long-term investments. The reason I do that is because it gives me an asset that can kick back money, meaning that I'll never go broke (as long as I have that long-term asset). For example, say you invest long term into Verizon and they kick out $5 a year per dividend yield per share. Say it costs $50 per share to buy in, and I have $5 million to put into the investment. That means I can buy 100,000 shares. If I hold those shares, they are going to pay me $500,000 a year—just for holding them. *That's* why you want to buy and invest in long-term investments.

And that's not even the best part. You can leverage that long-term investment to live off of that money. Let's look at our Verizon example again. Say I made $3 million in a year from short-term trading, and I only want to live off of $1.5 million of that. I can put the other $1.5 million into my long-term portfolio. Now say I want to live off of more than that $1.5 million, but I don't want to spend the $500,000 dividend because I want to keep reinvesting it. Why? Because if I have $5 million in there and I reinvest the $500,000, I now have $5.5 million in that account, which will earn me more dividend the following year. What I can do instead is leverage that account, meaning I can take a line of credit out on the five-year $5.5 million account. In fact, I can take up to 65 percent of that $5.5 million. I don't even have to sell the Verizon stock; I just borrow against it. I can borrow $3 million of that money at about 2 percent interest *which I then pay back to myself.*

A smart cookie will take that money and invest it into another asset, such as a real estate investment. Again, why? Say you buy a building with that $3 million you took out, so you don't have any loans against the building, and it kicks out 10 percent a year, giving you another $300,000. Now you have $300,000 coming out of that real estate asset *and* $500,000 coming out of that Verizon stock. What you do is keep reinvesting in Verizon because now, in year two, you are getting a little bit more than $500,000 since you reinvested the $500,000 from year one. Each year you reinvest, you'll make a little more (in year two, you'll get about $550,000, and in year three, you'll get $605,000). Now you can use $100,000 from the $300,000 you got from your real estate to slowly pay back the line of credit on your Verizon stock (at two percent, your payment will be just under $100,000). That leaves you $200,000 of free money to play with. You get to have fun while your money continues to grow. This is why they say the rich get richer. It's not just because they have the money to invest in the first place but because they also have the information on how to do it correctly. Ninety-five percent of the world doesn't know any of this.

I learned it ten years ago from a billionaire fitness client. He's the one who taught me the saying "When's the best time to sell an asset? Never." If your asset is making you money, you never sell it. This applies to your long-term investments: your real estate, your art, and your diamonds, gold, and silver. You get it, you keep it, and you hold it forever.

Hedge Funds

I like hedge funds a little better than mutual funds. Now, I'm going to preface this by saying I can't claim this 100 percent, but I don't know of any mutual funds that bet against the market. When you short the stock market and it falls, you make money. No mutual funds or ETFs that I know of do that, but a hedge fund can. A hedge fund's principal goal is to beat the market. That's it. It doesn't matter how you beat the market, as long as you beat it. If the market is doing 20 percent this year, a hedge fund needs to do 30 or 40 percent. If the market is at 50 percent, it needs to do 80 or 100 percent.

The downside is that while you are beating the market, you have to give them "2–20." That means giving them a 2 percent management fee *and* 20 percent of the money they helped you make. This can be good for someone who is a working professional who likes what they do and doesn't have time to manage their own portfolio. This person just wants to put their money somewhere and let it grow passively. A hedge fund, especially a good hedge fund, is a good way to do that. However, with a hedge fund, if you are looking at the market and nothing looks good right now, so you want to sit on the money and wait for a good buying opportunity: tough luck. You cannot do that in a hedge fund. The rule is that the fund money must always be working. No good buying opportunities? Oh well, you gotta buy something anyway.

LET'S TALK ABOUT SAVINGS ACCOUNTS

Stock isn't the only way to earn passive income. There are other options such as 401(k)s, IRAs, pension plans, and social security. Let's look at each of them.

401(k)s

Personally, I think 401(k)s are a scam. They can be beneficial for people who don't want to put time and effort into learning the markets and crypto and investing, however. If you like your job and never want to quit, and if you don't want to focus on building your own business, then contribute to your 401(k). Hopefully, your company will match your contribution. Even if they don't, add the max amount of money into your account each year until you are ready to retire and leave your job.

401(k)s are self-run passively, which means the returns won't be as good as if you were to get in there and do a little work yourself. The less you touch your money, the less money you will make. That's why I prefer stocks because if you do your own research and trade your own stocks, you can make a lot more money. You also don't have to deal with fees when you handle your own stocks. With 401(k)s, the money you make isn't all yours. You have to pay fees when you pull money out. In a nutshell, I don't suggest investing in a 401(k) when you can put in a little effort and make a lot more money in stocks. A 401(k) is never going to get you to F-U Money (which is the whole point of reading this book, right?).

IRAs

Similar to 401(k)s, IRAs are good if you like your job and want to stay there. However, if you own your business or are self-employed, you can do an SEP-IRA (Simplified Employee Pension plan) instead. Just know that if you have any employees, you must contribute the same amount of money for each of them as you put in for yourself. A traditional IRA lets you contribute up to $6,000 a year. An SEP-IRA lets you contribute up to 25 percent of your yearly compensation (of course, it is the government, so there's a few extra catches in there, but that's the general gist).[8] The good thing about IRAs is that you can put your IRA money into stocks, and IRAs let you pick *which* stocks to put that money into. The even better thing is that when you are ready to sell your stocks, you can sell them tax-free. That's because your money is taxed before you put it in the IRA, so everything accumulated there is tax-free.

---

8   Internal Revenue Service (IRS), *Simplified Employee Pension Plan (SEP)*, accessed December 9, 2021, https://www.irs.gov/retirement-plans/plan-sponsor/simplified-employee-pension-plan-sep.

Pension Plans

I'll be honest. I have no fucking idea how these work. That's because they are old and antiquated. My generation knows that we are never going to make any money out of a pension plan, so we haven't paid attention to it. Why waste our brain power or energy learning something we'll never get to use? You either have time or money, and learning about pension plans is going to waste your time while not earning you any money.

Social Security

Guess what! We're never going to see a penny from social security either. That shit is going to be bankrupt well before we retire. Don't waste your time.

AVERAGE RETURNS

Now you know you want to put your money into a passive vehicle that earns you money while you sleep. Great. Smart. But how much return are these vehicles *actually* going to give you in a year?

- Mutual funds: 10 to 15 percent a year (but once all those fees come out, you're looking at closer to 6 percent)

- ETF (exchange-traded funds): 5 to 8 percent a year

- Index funds: 10 to 15 percent a year

- Long-term investing in quality companies: 15 to 30 percent a year (you have to do research on what companies to invest in, and know that some years you might do 50 percent and some years you may do 5 percent)

- Hedge funds: 20 to 100 percent a year

- 401(k)s: 2 to 6 percent a year (less once the fees come out)

- IRAs: done right, you can do 10 to 20 percent a year; done wrong, you'll either lose or make 5 to 7 percent a year

I personally don't have a 401(k), hedge fund, or mutual fund. I have one index fund.

Where I make a lot of my money is through long-term investing in quality companies. If you find the right quality companies that are staged the correct way, these companies will have the ability to have a 50x to 100x growth over twenty or thirty years. So if you put $10,000 into stock in one quality company, you don't touch it for twenty years, and it has 100x return, you just made a million dollars. Ten grand into one million with no work on your part. You just made a good bet.

The hard part is finding the right companies to invest in. I have good instincts—but I do a *lot* of homework. My lady will tell you I'm a fucking maniac. I eat, breathe, and live stocks. When I wake up in the morning, the first thing I do is look at stock charts. I go through companies' balance sheets. I watch CNBC all day long. (I literally put it on the TV, and it stays on all day long.) On the rare occasion I watch a movie or show, it's a stock-related movie, like *The Big Short, Billions,* or *Wall Street.* I listen to stock podcasts. (A great podcast to start with is mine, of course: *Get to the Bag.* Others that I love are *The Rich Dad Radio Show* and the *BiggerPockets* podcast.)

I do this all day, every day. I've made it my life. I am obsessed. And it has made me filthy rich.

PLAYING THE GAME

The stock market is like a game. If you get it right, you make a lot of money. There are two ways to play the stock market. One is the long-term game; it's a slow one. You have to wait ten, twenty, or even thirty years to see if you played your cards right. You just invest in your brokerage account every month and let it sit. Ideally, you forget about it.

A brokerage firm did a study that looked at two groups of customers: one group logged into their accounts at least once a month, and the other group never logged into their account (they either lost their password or they died—morbid, I know).

The accounts of the people who never logged in performed much better than the other group. In short: Don't. Touch. Your. Account. You only need about $200 to get started in long-term stock investing.

The second game is the short game: day trading. This game is the epitome of high risk, high reward. If you play your cards right, you can make 100, 200, or even 500 percent return in a single month. It allows you to beat the market at a higher rate. However, it's harder to do. In fact, most people can't do it. They will lose. If you get good at it, if you watch the market and know what to look for, you can beat the market every year. It just takes a lot more of your concentration and dedication. To start day trading, you need a minimum of $2,000. Why? Because you never want to put all your eggs (or money, in this case) in one basket. Never, ever put all your pennies in one stock, one trade, or one option. You should always hedge your bets to protect your investments.

In 2021, I beat the market by 240 percent. If you watch the market as much as I do, you can day trade. (Shameless plug here. If you don't know how to get started, I have a course called Secure The Bag that can teach you how to day trade correctly so you can beat the market and make money.)

STOCK MARKET CRASHES ARE GREAT FOR YOU

The stock market gets a bad rap about destroying lives when it crashes. However, as a trader, I see stock market crashes as a great opportunity. A crash is only a bad thing for people who don't know what the hell they are doing. When a stock market crashes, everything gets cheaper, enabling you to get stock essentially on sale. Plus, if you know what you are doing, you can see the signs of a crash before it happens and will know how to ride it out. When the market crashed in 2020, I made a lot of money as the market was falling. You just have to know how to play the game.

Historically speaking, crashes are known as a wealth exchange. It's when millionaires and billionaires are made because when someone is losing money, someone is making money on the other side. In 2020, I was already a millionaire with a net worth of maybe $2 million. Thanks to the crash, I left 2020 with a net worth of $32 million. I made $30 million in just one year. I know one guy who had $26 million at the start of a crash, and he came out the other side with $2.6 billion.

I was able to scoop up stocks at rock-bottom prices, sure. But I was also able to see the signs as the stock was going down and play against it with shorts. When you go short, you are making a bet that the stock you are shorting is going to fall below a certain number. For instance, if the stock is at $300 and you short it, you are saying, "I bet the stock is going to go under $300." And for every dollar it goes under, you make money.

However, while day trading is rewarding, it is very risky. You have to be very good at the game. I've seen people make stupid calls and lose a lot of money.

One day, I was doing an Instagram Live, giving out free advice (because I have the time and money, now that I have F-U Money, to give back) on what stocks to avoid. One of those stocks was Tesla. At the time, the Tesla stock was moving up like crazy, and a lot of people were getting FOMO (fear of missing out). However, I told my followers, "Don't go there. I am looking at their total stock chart, and it's not going to keep going."

Well, some people thought it would keep going, while I went against it, and started shorting Tesla. I ended up making $98,000 by shorting Tesla. Soon after, I heard from a guy who said, "Hey, you were right. You told me not to buy Tesla stock, and I did anyway."

So I asked him, "How much money did you lose?"

He said, "I lost $97,000." He lost over $90,000 when he could have paid me $15,000 to take my stock program, where I would have had him on the right side of that trade, allowing him to make money instead of losing it. But he, like a lot of people, didn't want to pay for help. He wanted to DIY it and ended up losing big time. Don't learn this lesson the hard way. Pay for help, whether it's coaching to build your business or a program like mine that helps you learn how to day trade.

TIPS FROM TAY

This chapter is why you needed to do all the steps in the previous chapter. This is why you needed to stop having kids. Instead of spending $15,000 a year toward a kid, you can put that $15,000 toward the stock market. This is why you need to stop drinking, smoking, and partying. You can put all that wasted money into the stock market. It's not just about not spending your money. It's about actively investing it into the right vehicles in order to make a return.

By choosing not to drink, smoke, have sex, and party, you are actively building your discipline muscle. (Yes, discipline is a muscle, and you need to work it to get it stronger.) You're a more disciplined entrepreneur because you've been practicing by not wasting your time or money. Once you have a business, you can continue to build that muscle by extending its use to help ensure you run a healthy company. You learn what a balance sheet is, what an income statement is, and how to track the health of your business, so you know if your company is doing well or not. Then when you get to the stock market, you aren't new to assessing companies because you've been assessing your own company for years. You'll be a better stock picker because you know what a healthy company looks like. Everything you've done up to this point is helping set you up to be good at investing in the stock market.

The stock market is going to be the fastest way to freedom and F-U Money. I went from $2 million to $32 million. Two million might not be considered F-U Money by a lot of people, but $32 million sure as fuck is. The lesson of the chapter is: don't waste your money on kids, booze, and 401(k)s. Pay to learn the shortcut of the stock market, invest your money correctly, and take the fast lane to F-U Money.

Before moving on, ask yourself these questions:

Does this feel like something that will be helpful on your journey?

If yes, in what specific way could you see this being helpful?

How does this fit (or not fit) into your GPS?

11

CRYPTOCURRENCY

TIPTOEING INTO DIGITAL MONEY

Crypto is risky and volatile right now, but it's the future. Get used to it.

You could say I'm one of the lucky ones who invested into Bitcoin early, but really, I did my homework.

The first time I heard about Bitcoin was when I read an article about a guy who spent 10,000 bitcoins for Papa John's to deliver a pizza. They ended up calling it the $630 million pizza. This was back when Bitcoin was $0.004 per coin at the time—not even a penny. The guy's pizza was $41. He was so excited that the financial system was advancing that he went out on a limb and decided, "Hey, I'm going to pay for these pizzas in Bitcoin." If he had held on to that Bitcoin, it'd be worth $630 million today.

This was back around 2011, when crypto was the Wild, Wild West (let's be real, it still is). At the time, people were getting bitcoins stolen out of their wallets, and I'm thinking, *Yeah, I don't want to deal with this shit. No, thank you.* I didn't think about it again until 2017 when Bitcoin skyrocketed to $20,000 per coin. That's when I thought, *Holy shit,* and I started watching it closely. I decided if it dipped back down, I'd buy it. In the meantime, I did the same smart thing I did for stocks and started researching it.

Once I knew what was going on and it dropped back down to $5,000 per coin in 2019, I decided to grab it. I spent a little over $150,000 to get 30 coins.

Then I started hearing about another type of coin called Ethereum. So I said to myself, "Alright, let's do some research." I read articles, and I watched YouTube videos from people who were experts in the cryptocurrency space. What they said made sense, so I decided to invest in Ethereum as well and spent $40,000 to buy roughly 100 coins. After about ten months, Bitcoin hit around $8,000 a coin, so I sold almost all of it, just in case it was a fluke. That was about $200,000 in profit in a year. In the same period, Ethereum went from about $300 a coin to about $4,000 a coin—so I sold 43 of those coins too and made $85,000. I held on to the other 57 coins and sold them later for a profit for $188,000.

I had a good experience with crypto. However, as I study it more, I realize it's still in its infancy stage. Apple stock is worth $2.4 trillion. Every type of crypto *combined* isn't worth that much.

When one company in the stock market is worth more than the entire cryptocurrency world, then crypto has a long way to go.

I'm going to make a prediction here at the end of 2021 while I'm writing this book. I think Bitcoin is going to reach between $85,000 and $100,000, crash, and then pull back to somewhere around or under $20,000.

THE MONEY VERSION OF THE INTERNET

Crypto is the money version of the internet.

In 1995, the mass population was introduced to the internet, and the start of the dot-com bubble began. Every internet stock went sky-high, but eventually, the bubble inflated so big that it popped. About 90 percent of internet companies went bankrupt. The ones who survived were the ones who had staying power, such as Amazon and Apple, and ended up thriving in the post-dot-com world.

Crypto is going to be a repetition of history. The stock market has several cycles that it repeats over time: there's a one-hundred-year cycle, ninety-year cycle, twenty-year cycle, and eight- to ten-year cycle.

The internet and stock market aren't the only things that go through cycles. There's a hundred-year cycle where you see a repeating of things in history, such as the Spanish flu in the 1920s, which was eerily similar to COVID-19. They were doing the same things we are now, such as wearing face masks and mandating where and when people could travel. Also, during the Roaring Twenties, there was a lack of free speech. You couldn't say certain things because it could hurt people's feelings (cue the eye roll). There was also a boom in the LGBTQ+ community, where people were coming out. It was a massive time for entrepreneurs who were making a lot of money. The stock market was under a ten-year bull cycle. A car company was making groundbreaking moves (a.k.a. Ford). Today, we have Elon Musk with Tesla who is the modern-day Ford.

Every eight to ten years, there will be some time of recession, whether it's a collapse or a down economy. We saw it happen in 1992, around 2000, obviously 2008 (which lasted until 2010), and the most recent one in 2020. That puts us at 2028 to 2030 for the next crash.

With crypto, I'm predicting a twenty-year cycle. Of the over three thousand cryptocurrencies currently in existence, about 90 percent of them will go bankrupt in twenty years.

This is the risk you take investing in crypto. There is no telling which companies are going to make it. However, with research, you can hedge your bets and (try to) predict which ones you think will. For instance, I don't think Bitcoin or Ethereum are going anywhere. My advice: tread lightly. Don't put all your money in crypto, and be sure to watch the trends carefully. In fact, you shouldn't even touch crypto until you are doing well in the stock market.

DON'T SUCCUMB TO FOMO

I know that crypto is the new, hot thing that everyone is screaming about, but don't invest just because it's popular. It's true there are massive opportunities out there. There is one called Sheba that was worth $0.00032 when it first launched. If you had put $100 into this coin at the beginning of 2021, at the end of 2021, you would have $60 million. It's unbelievable—but many of these companies and coins are gambles. There's no real history to review or study or learn from because it's so new. You don't know what's going to go up or what's going to fizzle out.

In fact, it's so new that it isn't fully regulated. This means there's opportunity for seasoned, knowledgeable investors to come in and manipulate the market against people who have no clue of what they're doing. In late 2021, Elon Musk was able to artificially inflate certain cryptocurrencies just by talking about them. No one can prove he did it on purpose, but it still blew up because he talked about it. If he had put $1 million into a coin before talking about it, he could've easily turned that into several hundred million dollars in just a few days.

In the stock market, there are rules in place to keep people from doing just that. If I went online and said, "Hey this stock is doing great; come buy it," and it went up and I sold, the SEC would lock my ass up in a heartbeat. Crypto has no safety regulations—it's the Wild, Wild West. While the IRS and FTC are trying to get regulations in place, there's nothing in place now, so you have to be careful you don't get played.

THE COIN OF CHOICE

If I had to choose a coin to back, it would be Bitcoin. First, it's proving itself to be something that will store the value of your money. In other words, inflation won't affect the value of your dollar if it's invested in Bitcoin. If you had $10 million in cash at the start of 2021, at the end of the year, you'd have lost 5 percent of that due to inflation. If you had $10 million in Bitcoin at the start of 2021, at the end of the year, it would have gone up 300 percent. Bitcoin is essentially a hedge against inflation.

Second, you can get your money out in minutes with no hassle. If you need to get $200,000 out of the bank, and you go to the bank to ask for it in cash, they won't give it to you. You have to jump through hoop after hoop before you can get your own money—and you have to pay a fee to get it! With Bitcoin, if your family member needs cash immediately, you can send them a code, and in five minutes, they'll have the money, no transaction fees attached.

Third (and this is my favorite thing), if I need to get myself or my family out of the city, state, or country *fast*, I can't take $10 million in cash with me. I also can't take it in gold—that shit is fucking heavy, and in this hypothetical situation, I don't have time to rent a truck. But I can take $10 million in Bitcoin. I can put that on a flash drive, throw it in my pocket, and go across the world.

Fourth, it's decentralized. You don't have to worry about banks or governments telling you what you can or cannot do with your money. Bitcoin can be cashed in for pretty much anything and exchanged into any other physical currency: dollar, euro, yen, pound, etc. It's universally recognized as well, so in most countries, you can use it as is.

TIPS FROM TAY

For your homework, I want you to do some research. Look into the history of Bitcoin and Ethereum. Where did they start, how much have they grown year over year, and how are they doing right now?

Now that you have that knowledge, *don't do anything*.

Right now, crypto is too crazy. If you do your research as I suggest above, you'll see there's not enough history to it. You can't look at it, see what it's done in the past, and know what cycles to predict. For me, I really like to invest in companies that are not going anywhere (think Google, Amazon, Microsoft, Apple). I see crypto disappearing before Apple, Amazon, or Microsoft. That's just common sense.

However, if you have a handsome amount of disposable income and you've done your research, you could put some money, maybe 20 percent, into crypto. Know that this is a gamble. Putting all your money into crypto because you're hoping to catch the next Dogecoin is financial suicide.

Before moving on, ask yourself these questions:

Does this feel like something that will be helpful on your journey?

If yes, in what specific way could you see this being helpful?

How does this fit (or not fit) into your GPS?

12

REAL ESTATE

It takes more upfront money to get into real estate. When paying so much, it's good that you can actually touch it.

I was nineteen years old the first time I failed at real estate. This was before I started my company, while I was still working at the warehouse. I decided to attempt house hacking—you buy a house, move your entire family in with you, and everyone splits the bills so that the house can be paid off on an accelerated timeline.

Once the home is paid off, you buy another house, move the entire family, and rent out the first house. Now, all the rent you are making on the first home is profit because it's fully paid off, plus you are still paying less money for bills because everyone is chipping in. When done right, it's a great method to get into real estate and help the entire family level up faster.

However, it didn't quite work out the way I had hoped. I bought a $250,000, 3,000-square-foot, five-bedroom home in Nashville. I moved my family in. Everything was going great until several family members decided they would rather struggle financially in order to have their own place for "peace of mind" (cue my eye roll here). They were stuck in the mindset that living with other people meant they were pathetic. So, they left, and I was stuck with a 250K home I couldn't afford.

I was livid. I put my name on the line. I put my credit on the line. I put my well-being on the line. And my family abandoned me when I needed their support the most. The entire situation ended up with me losing the house and filing for bankruptcy.

That's a great first encounter with real estate, right? I tried to level up too quickly, without enough money, which is why I tell my clients that real estate isn't something you want to do until you have a lot of money. Learn from my (costly) mistake.

FOUR WAYS TO GET INTO REAL ESTATE

There are four main ways you can get into real estate, each one more costly than the last. We'll start on the method that costs the least and move toward the most costly (and potentially profitable) method.

Wholesaling: the Cheapest Way to Get into Real Estate

Wholesaling is the idea that you find a run-down home that needs a couple hundred thousand dollars' worth of renovation work. You then put a contract on the house. The catch here is that you don't plan to actually buy the house. Instead, you are just putting a contract on it, so you have the right to sell the contract to someone else who wants to buy it.

Putting a contract on the house essentially gets you first rights to the house. When you do, you generally get between thirty and sixty days for due diligence, which is when you can get it inspected, check the foundations, make sure you know what you are buying, etc. When you are wholesaling, this gives you thirty to sixty days to go out and shop for someone to buy it.

For example, say you put in a contract on a house being sold for $200,000. You know that you can put $40,000 into the house and the value will increase from $200,000 to $400,000. This new number is the after-renovation value or ARV.

Now you can go to other investors and say, "Hey, I have a contract on a $200,000 house. All you need to do is put in $40,000, and you can sell it for $400,000, which is a profit of $160,000." If the person is interested, you can tell them, "My assignment fee is only $30,000." If you have a deal, you just earned $30,000. Now, for some homes, you may have to put in earnest money to get the contract, but that's usually between $2,000–$5,000.

Occasionally, you may have to pay for an inspection, which is usually around $500. Other than that earnest and inspection money, this method costs you nothing. You can get started with wholesaling with less than $10,000.

You may be thinking, *This sounds great, I can definitely do this tomorrow.* Pump the brakes on that thought. I had it too, and it did not work great for me. When I first heard of wholesaling, I decided to give it a try. I found a house, put in a contract, paid my $2,000 of earnest money, and started my due diligence period. The unit ended up having a lot more wrong with it than I realized, and no one was ever going to buy it from me. I was still in my due diligence period, so I told the owner I wanted out. Legally, you as the buyer have the right to back out during this period and void the contract. Well, the owner came back and said, "You're wasting our time. We're going to sue you."

What the fuck, right?

Over the next few weeks, there was back-and-forth between my real estate agent and the seller, and they managed to get my agent on board with *them.* She came back to me and said, "Well, you did waste all of our time, and we all think you should buy this regardless of what's wrong with it."

I was pissed and a little panicked at this point because this was not how it was supposed to go. The whole point of due diligence is to be able to save your ass and get out of a contract. At this point in my life, I was not rich (I wasn't even close). I didn't have the money to hire a high-powered attorney. However, one of my *clients* was a high-powered attorney, and she jumped in the ring with me. She got involved and told them what they were doing was illegal, and they backed off real quick and voided the contract. I lucked all the way out.

I realized that wholesaling had its own huge headaches that came with it, and I decided then and there I was never going to do this again. Instead, I decided to wait until I had enough money to play at a higher level and to do it right. Next time, I would be able to afford my own high-powered attorney.

House Hacking—with a Twist

Let's talk house hacking next. Now, you may be thinking, *Tay, didn't this screw you already?* Yes, it did. However, there's a way to do it that doesn't involve buying a single-family home.

Say you qualify for a $500,000 house. Instead of buying a single-family home, you can buy a duplex or quad and rent out the other units. Now you have your own place you can live in, but you have one to three tenants paying you anywhere from $1,000–$2,000 a month. So if you buy a quad and you have three tenants paying $2,000 each, that's $6,000 a month to put on your $500,000 loan, which should only be around $2,500 a month (depending on your loan rates, down payments, etc.).[9] Now, not only are you living for free (because you are paying the

---

9 Note that this number will depend on how much money you put down and the loan rate.

loan with your tenants' rent), but you are also making around $3,500 a month that you can either invest or use to pay off the loan faster.

It's Time to Flip

Flipping costs a little more money. This is the most commonly talked about option in real estate. Normally, this is the person on the other side of a wholesale deal. Here's how this would work.

Lisa wants to do wholesaling. She goes out, finds a house, puts a contract on it, and finds the potential value. She then approaches Tay, who is a flipper, and tells him, "Hey, I know you flip homes. I found a home that if you put in $30,000, it'll make you $100,000." Tay agrees to the deal, pays the $20,000 assignment fee, and closes on the house. Now that he owns the house, he can bring in his contractors, roofers, and anyone else he needs to fix up the house and make it look pretty. Then, Tay sells it for a profit.

Flipping can be a great way to make money. However, it's very cash-intensive. Most banks won't loan you money to flip a house, so you must be able to pay for it in cash. And you must be able to get access to the cash quickly. In the flipping world, good deals move fast. After all, if someone is selling their house and they need to get out ASAP, who do you think they'll sell to? The person who has cash on them or the person who needs to wait thirty days for the bank?

Commercial Real Estate: Buying and Holding

This is the top rung on our ladder, where the big money is spent and made. Commercial real estate is often referred to as a buy-and-hold strategy because you buy it and never sell it. This takes the most amount of money to get started. For one, you want to be able to buy it and never sell it, so you can't need to be able to sell it fast. When you buy commercial property, you are looking for buildings with four, eight, sixteen, twenty, or one hundred units. (I've seen people who do this with a thousand units.) To get a building this size, you are going to need 20 to 30 percent down. For a hundred-unit property, it's going to cost at least $25 million. Twenty percent of that is going to be at least $5 million.

While this type of investment needs a lot more money than flipping or wholesaling, it is the method that I suggest you hold out for. Why? Because it comes with a lot of benefits. One is cash flow. If you have $5 million to put down on a property, that means it's just sitting in a bank, not doing anything, being eaten away by inflation. Instead, put that money down on the $25 million property. After everything is paid off—and I mean everything, the management team, your debt every month, all of it—and each of those hundred units is bringing you $100, that's $10,000 a month every month those units are filled. So you are looking at $120,000 a year on a $5 million investment. And this is a conservative estimate. Normally, you can make about $350,000 to $500,000 a year on a $5 million investment, but even if you are making $120,000, you're still making more than you would if that money was sitting in a bank.

Then, you can hold it forever. Over about fifteen years, the money you make from your tenants will pay off the entire $20 million owed on the property. Now, your units are earning $1,500 a month in rent (thanks to rent increases to keep up with inflation), with $500 of each unit paid to a team who runs the building, and you are making a profit of $1,000 per unit per month. That's $100,000 a month, for $1.2 million a year—for as long as you own the building (and the units are filled).

HOW TO USE PROPERTIES AS COLLATERAL FOR LOANS

I will never sell my real estate investments. If there ever came a time that I did want to cash in, instead of selling the property to get the money out, I can go to a bank and say, "Here's my collateral."

Banks will give you 70–80 percent loan to value. So, if you have $1 million and you get 80 percent loan value, you just got an $800,000 loan. The best part? Your tenants will be the ones to pay that loan off for you.

REAL ESTATE AS A WEALTH PRESERVATION TOOL

Over the last two hundred years, real estate has only gone up in value. The house you wanted five years ago costs a lot more today. The house you want today is going to cost more in ten years. If I buy a lot of properties and hold them until I die, my children will inherit them, and if they do it right, *their* children will inherit them. It's a tool you can use to keep your children's children wealthy.

Real estate also keeps your money safe from inflation. Inflation continues to go up, but real estate goes up more. Why? Because while the dollar gets cheaper, the value of real estate stays the same. No matter what happens to the dollar, your real estate investment will continue to increase.

Now, it's true that real estate could go down and the dollar could deflate (the opposite of inflate and inflation), and some property could lose value. However, the last two centuries have shown us that it's best to get into real estate if you want to preserve the wealth you have. The catch is that you have to have wealth to preserve. If you only have $100,000 or even $1 million, you don't really have a lot of wealth to preserve. First, you have to build the wealth (through entrepreneurship, then stock, and then crypto), and then you can start preserving it through real estate. (Funny how this is coming full circle, right?)

REAL ESTATE IS GREAT FOR CASH FLOW

There are three ways to get good cash flow. The first is entrepreneurship. If you have a business and you're running it well, it can provide good cash flow. However, it requires a shit-ton of people to run the business, and you have to pay them first.

The second way to get cash flow is by way of stocks that pay dividends. If you have $1 million stock and it pays five to ten dividends a year, you are getting paid $50,000 a year for doing nothing. The good thing about stock is that it doesn't come with headaches. There's no worry about employees or tenants. You don't have to worry about a property management team. It's literally just you and the stock. However, it doesn't give you any tax benefits.

The third way is through real estate. Yes, you have to worry about tenants and your property team, but you get a lot of cash flow, thanks to the people paying you to use your building every month. So even if you stay in bed all day (lazy ass), you are still making money. Plus, as discussed earlier, you get great tax benefits.

MY CURRENT REAL ESTATE INVESTMENTS

As of December 2021, I had four homes: three in the US and one in Puerto Rico. However, I didn't want to take out debt to get any of these homes, especially with the high inflation and uncertain times that were happening in 2021. Instead, I waited until I could pay cash for each of these properties.

For my Puerto Rico home, I paid $6 million in cash. It was a highly sought-after property, and it had a lot of bids on it. (I actually paid for it before it was even finished being built.) With so many people trying to get the place, they wanted to go with the person paying cash: me.

I was able to go into the deal aggressively and say, "Hey, I want this place. What will it take for me to get this place now? I'll wait for it to be finished, but I want to get the contract now."

They said, "If you pay 50 percent now and 50 percent when it's done, in cash, it's yours."

I said, "Great, I'll send you a wire tomorrow." Paying cash enabled me to skip the line and get the place I wanted before anyone else could (because they were waiting for approval from a bank).

The best part is that if I ever want to leverage it, it's already paid off. I can go to a bank and get an equity line of credit for up to 50 percent of the value as a loan. If I wanted to, I could take out $3 million against it right now and use that money to buy another piece of property, put it in the stock market, or live off of it. This is why it's so important to have cash before you get into real estate. It enables you to move fast and increase your net worth. Now, I realize I'm using big numbers for my examples, but you can do this with $500,000. Buy a $500,000 house in cash, take a 50 percent loan on it, and put $250,000 into the stock market or buy another property that you can rent out. Then you make money twice over.

The trick is knowing what you want out of it. For me, $500,000 wasn't enough. Instead, I kept investing, kept saving, and waited until I had enough for me to get the exact house I wanted.

It is one of the most freeing things in the world to be able to pay cash for a $6 million house. Especially when you come from a background like mine. When you don't know how you are going to be able to pay the rent, keep the lights on, or have running water, it consumes your entire day.

People will ask you, "Why aren't you happy? Why aren't you smiling? Why don't you study more?" And a lot of the time, it was because my mind was occupied with thinking, *How am I going to pay my bills today?*

Worrying about bills, worrying about how you are going to pay things, and worrying about where your next dollar will come from can dramatically decrease the value of your life because you can't do a single thing without thinking about it.

Now I can relax. Now I don't have to stress. Now I know where my dollars are coming from, and I know I can pay my bills. Now that I'm not thinking about all that, I have the freedom to think about what else I want to do. And I can go do it. I can enhance myself. Right now, I'm learning Spanish, and when I'm fluent, I'm going to learn French. When you don't have to worry about where your next dollar will come from, you can free up your mind to learn new things, enhance your life, and make yourself a better person. (After all, who doesn't want to speak multiple languages?)

Freedom can be dangerous and lull you into a sense of security though. If you start thinking, *Oh, I don't have to pay the mortgage or rent. I just have to keep the lights on and feed myself, pay some property taxes, and that's it,* then you might start becoming complacent. You might start taking your foot off the gas because you don't think you have to work for it anymore. You need to make sure you still have some type of motivation to keep you moving forward. Don't let yourself slack off.

TIPS FROM TAY

Real estate should be your last method of investing. You need a lot of upfront capital to make it work, but then your money will work for you and save you a lot of money on your taxes.

There are also incentives across the world where countries or islands will give you tax benefits to live there. For instance, because I bought my house in Puerto Rico, I pay 0 percent on capital gains while I'm living in that house. The catch being that I have to physically live there six months out of the year. While I do, I pay basically nothing in taxes on any money I make while I'm there.

Do your own research to see where you can buy property and save on your taxes. However, know that you can't try to save on taxes until you have a substantial amount of money. To move to Puerto Rico and save on taxes, you have to buy a house. And houses in Puerto Rico cost more than houses in Miami. My $6 million home in PR is only 4,000 square feet. For that amount in Miami, I can get an *8,000*-square-foot home (but I'd have to pay a lot more in taxes).

Tax rules change all the time. See what tax rules are currently in play. (But really, do the research once you have already made a lot of money through your business and the stock market.)

Before moving on, ask yourself the following questions:

Does this feel like something that will be helpful on your journey?

If yes, in what specific way could you see this being helpful?

How does this fit (or not fit) into your GPS?

13

THE CYCLONE OF MONEY

MONEY IS CURRENCY

When I was poor, all the nice things we liked and could afford were liabilities that mostly went down in value. When I reached F-U Money, I learned that most of the nice things that more well-off people like are assets and tend to go up in value even as they use them.

Before you can make money, you first must understand that money is currency. I don't mean currency as in a system of money; I mean currency as in an electric current. An electric current is always moving—and your money should be too.

When I was twenty years old, I heard someone say, "currency, currency, currency." At the time, I wasn't sure if he was saying currency as in money or as in electricity. That's when it clicked in my mind that there is no difference. Both money and electricity have to move to be able to provide benefits. If you want lights in your house, electricity has to move through wires and into light bulbs so you can have the benefit of light. It's the same principle with money. You have to move your currency and keep it moving so that you can get the benefit of the money you have.

True players of this financial game move their currency through all four vehicles. When done right, each vehicle can raise enough money to buy something extra in the next vehicle.

Once you make your F-U Money, you shouldn't just have fun and let your money sit around, because that's how you lose. If you let it sit in a savings account, you're losing money. You need to take that money and move it into stock, and then into real estate, and then into crypto so you can get the full benefits.

Once you understand this idea of money as currency, you'll realize like I did that you have to keep your money moving until the day you die. You can't just stop and be done with it. Once you make a few million, it's not over. It may get easier for you to make money. It may make it easier for you to live the life you want to live. But the act of making and moving money doesn't stop. It's like they say, "If you're not living, you're dying," or "If you're not moving forward, you're moving backward." If you don't keep your money moving, you're going to start *losing* that money.

My move to Puerto Rico wasn't just for fun—it was a job. Sure, it's Puerto Rico and it's basically paradise, but I still had to work. I packed up my whole life to move there to keep my money moving. I had to change my way of thinking to island-life thinking. No, not what color tiny umbrellas I want in my drink or which lounge chair I want to lay in. I have to worry about hurricanes and be ready to fly myself and my family out at any given moment. (Another reason to invest in crypto and stock—they can easily come with me during an evacuation.)

When you get to a certain level, it's not just about making money anymore. It's about keeping money, and you have to work to do both. To fully optimize your F-U Money, you need to iterate your revenue streams.

EVERY VEHICLE FEEDS INTO THE OTHER

You want each wealth vehicle you use to feed into another one. You don't want to start with real estate, and you don't want to go directly into crypto, which is a gamble. Instead, you should start with entrepreneurship, especially if you are starting with little to no money. Then, instead of spending your money (or blowing it in the club showing off), you put your money in the stock market. The stock market, when done right, should be doubling or tripling your money. At this point, you should have enough money to gamble a little bit—i.e., going into crypto—or you can start investing into wealth preservation methods, such as real estate. All of these methods feed into the next, and, when done properly, end up looking like a cyclone.

The good news is that the cyclone doesn't stop there. There are several ways that enable you to keep your money cyclone moving. The first is buying art. You can buy a piece of art today, and in five to ten years, it'll double in value. The second is buying jewelry. For instance, in India, they buy their women a lot of gold jewelry, so if the husband dies, the woman has plenty of wealth around her arms, fingers, and neck to survive. The third is diamonds. Diamonds allow you to move large amounts of money without being spotted and with ease, just by carrying a bag in your pocket.

Of course, there are more than these three, and when you get to this point in your F-U Money journey, you can start to research which wealth preservation methods are best for you.

DON'T HAVE MULTIPLE STREAMS OF REVENUE

I don't believe in moving into multiple streams of revenue too fast. Instead, you should determine which one is the most beneficial and iterate it. That means improving the stream that is bringing you the most money and cutting the rest.

When you move into multiple streams too quickly, your first streams fail. For instance, say you have one stream of income that's making you $100,000 a year. You get excited and start a second and third stream. To do that, you take your attention away from the first stream to focus on the others. Now the second and third streams are making you about $10,000 each a year, for an extra $20,000 total a year. However, because you split so much of your attention between the three streams of income, that first stream was neglected, and it's no longer making you $100,000 a year. Instead, it's only making you $50,000 a year. Now, instead of making $100,000 a year with your original stream of income, you're only making $70,000 a year with three.

I did this with my personal training business. I was making really good money as a trainer, upward of $100,000 a year. However, I tried to get ahead of myself and created other streams of revenue. I was trying to come up with products, services, and other forms of income because that's what I thought I was supposed to do. What really happened, however, is that I started losing money from my training business. You don't want to take your eye off something that is making you a lot of money in an attempt to make money somewhere else—especially when that stream is working. Instead, focus on just that one stream so you can optimize it and continue to make more and more.

How do you know which revenue streams to focus on and which ones to cut? By checking the numbers. If one stream is bringing you 10 percent a year, and the other is bringing you 30 percent a year, you should double down on the 30 percent one and stop working on the 10 percent one.

WEALTH PRESERVATION IN TIMES OF INFLATION

Investing in art, jewelry, and diamonds is always a good idea, but especially in times of inflation. Gold, silver, and other precious metals are also a good investment idea because they are resources. For instance, most space equipment requires gold as a component in order to work. As space exploration continues to grow, the demand for gold is only going to increase. Silver and nickel are both used to build batteries for electric vehicles. Another item that's only growing in demand.

Not only are these metals and jewels essential to create items we use in daily life, but they are also something that people just absolutely love. No matter how bad things get, people are always going to love and appreciate the beauty of diamonds. They're shiny, they're beautiful, and they make us happy. Jewels were also historically used for dowries so that if something happened to their husbands, women could sell their jewelry to survive. They are also easy to take with you if you need to leave a place quickly, thanks to their (generally) lightweight nature. Just put your diamonds in a bag (or as the many historical figures did, sew them into the lining of your clothes) and go. Or you can keep them in a safe-deposit box.

LIFE INSURANCE AS AN ASSET

Most people don't consider life insurance as an asset, but it is. While it may not be an asset to you personally while you are alive, it's definitely an asset to your estate or family. If there's one sure bet you can make in life, it's that you are going to die. So you should prepare while you are alive.

To be clear, I'm not talking about term life insurance. Term life insurance is what it sounds like. You are paying for a term of your life. It's not something you pay indefinitely. It's not something that you're going to get cash value in. If you pay on it, and you die within that term, then you get the value of that life insurance. If you don't, then that is just money flushed down the toilet.

The real asset I'm talking about is whole life insurance. You want insurance that you get cash value for. Now, this will be a little pricier to set up; however, it allows you to accrue money and value on your policy as long as you're alive. Most insurance companies offer a yearly return of around 4 percent. And the best part is that you can use the value of your policy while you're alive by borrowing against it.

Another benefit is that whole life insurance is tax-free. Not only when it is claimed after you die but also when you borrow against it or if you withdraw from it (so long as you use it for retirement). It's essentially a tax loophole.

WHY ALL THIS MATTERS

When you get to a certain point of financial success and literacy, you'll notice that a lot of times, individuals end up with more money than they know what to do with or need. Say a person needs $200,000 a year for their lifestyle. That gets them a nice home, the ability to travel six to ten times a year, and the freedom to enjoy themselves. Well, once people get their finances figured out, this person who only needs $200,000 is making $1 million, $800,000 more than they know what to do with. There are two types of people in this situation. One person is going to take that $800,000 and put it in a bank and sit on it. The other person is going to put that $800,000 to work. Invested properly over eight to ten years, $800,000 will turn into roughly $2 million. Meanwhile, the person who saved the $800,000 still has $800,000 if they didn't touch it.

THE IMPORTANCE OF APPRECIATING ASSETS

When you make a certain amount of money, you need to consider appreciating assets, especially ones that do well in higher inflationary times, such as precious metals and collectibles.

For example, when I first bought my Lamborghini, a lot of people went crazy, saying, "Oh my God! Why would you pay that much for a depreciating asset? As soon as you drive it off the lot, it's going to go down in value. That doesn't make sense." Before you reach a certain amount of money at a certain level, buying a Lamborghini doesn't make sense, because you believe anything that has four wheels and is used for transportation is a depreciating liability. However, a Lamborghini is a collectible. In fact, mine went up in value almost 40 percent in a year.

People believe the same thing when it comes to Rolexes. They say, "Why would I pay $50,000 for a logo? I have the same watch that tells the same time that only costs $20. If I want to be fancy, I can get a gold one for $100." Again, people don't realize the market value when it comes to collectibles. My $50,000 Rolex watch is now worth $85,000.

There's a whole different market that we aren't introduced to at lower levels. At low levels, we tend to think about all kinds of a thing being the same. However, there's a Chanel bag that was $5,000 when it first came out. Now, you'd have to pay $15,000 for it because it's a collectible, and there's a high demand and low supply.

THE CYCLONE OF MONEY

There is a different way of maneuvering that most of us are not introduced to at lower levels of earnings, and I have been trying to help people understand this since 2016.

One of the reasons I wanted to teach people financial education was because everyone I came across didn't want to just make it and be middle class. If you approach the average person and ask, "Do you want to be middle class, or do you want to be rich?" They are all going to say rich. I felt there was a need to teach people some of these guidelines on what it takes to get out of the lower or middle class to get rich. No one else was teaching this. There are people who teach how to live a debt-free, middle-class lifestyle for thirty to fifty years until you retire, and then you could be upper-middle class. Maybe, if you're lucky, even close to being rich. But to do that, you have to live debt-free, you have to get rid of those credit cards, and you gotta work the same job you hate for forty years.

I don't want to say that's not helpful, because it is for a lot of people. However, it's like I shouldn't be practicing basketball dribbling drills if I'm going to play football. You need specific training for your specific goals, and no one was teaching training on how to be rich. The goals of your money should be specific to the outcome you're looking for.

So many people teach "Stay debt-free, stay debt-free." However, I wanted to show people that the way many people, myself included, got rich was by borrowing money and using it to make more money. Why use my money to get rich when I can use other people's money?

I started with a podcast, and then it leaked over into a small group training. Then it evolved into a bigger group because so many people wanted to learn this knowledge. As word spread, it grew and grew from hundreds of people to thousands of people. Today, I offer what I like to call an online college course that allows you to move at your own pace by following along with prerecorded videos that teach the basics of what you've learned in this book and then elevate it. Then, once a week, there's a live class where I'll talk about how to level up in different types of vehicles, such as how to buy real estate without having to sell your current assets.

This is one place where collectibles come in handy. Say I want to buy a $2 million property, which will net me $100,000–$200,000 a year, and I need 20 percent down, which is $400,000. Instead of going to the bank and selling some of my stock, I can take a loan against my Lamborghini because it's worth $1 million. They'll let me take up to 80 percent of what it's worth. That's $600,000 that you can put into the property, which will pay back the money you borrowed, and now you have the $2 million property *and* your Lamborghini. My course teaches you both these tips and how to create one successful revenue stream at a time. (If you want to check out my course, go to https://stbwithtay.com.)

People always ask me why I'm giving my "secrets" away. My billionaire client took the time when I was twenty-two to show me how to get rich. He didn't charge me; he just did it out of the kindness of his heart. For me, this is paying it forward. I was taught at a young age one of the biggest purposes of man is to help their fellow man. One of the things that keeps us vibrant, alive, thriving, and mentally healthy along our own journey is helping other people. Another is knowing that there are always more people to help. In 2022, I was briefly hospitalized due to COVID-19. One of the things that helped get me out of the hospital and motivated me to get healthy again was knowing I had more people to help. I told myself I couldn't die yet because I had more people to help.

I truly believe my life's calling is to help other people be better versions of themselves. At first, it started with health, nutrition, and physical fitness. I helped people get healthier and be better parents for their children by living longer, thanks to improved health. That evolved as I entered my thirties and started helping people with their financial health. Helping improve the quality of people's lives keeps me going.

TIPS FROM TAY

There are many things that you can do with money that are somewhat smart. But there are many more ways outside of your traditional ways of investing or being a good shepherd of your money, which is why I created the cyclone of money. We've been taught that mutual funds, the stock market, and real estate are traditional ways of being a good shepherd of your money to grow to the next level.

While real estate is a good way to preserve your wealth, there are *other* ways to preserve it. In fact, when it comes to collectibles, there are actually a few things that have outpaced real estate and the stock market. For instance, the solid gold Rolex Daytona watch from 1957 has outpaced the stock market and real estate, percentagewise, along with most of your traditional assets, over the last sixty years.

The cycle of money is about alternative ways of appreciating your dollar. There are plenty. Honestly, the rabbit hole goes deep. Some parents have gotten on their kids for buying and playing with Pokémon cards. There are collectible cards now that you could have paid $10 for a pack, and one of those cards in that pack is now worth $30,000. That's crazy appreciation. It's also another great example of something outpacing the stock market. You can't put $10 into the stock market and make $30,000.

There are so many different collectibles. Write down a list of collectibles you like or are interested in.

One can be a Chanel purse, if you're into designer handbags. If you're into basketball, you can collect cards that you can hold on to as collectibles. Michael Jordan's rookie card, which originally cost about $5, appreciated to about $500,000. The first line of Michael Jordan shoes is going for $30,000. No signatures needed, just the plain shoes. The cyclone of money can be plugged into your interests and hobbies. It takes some work and some investigation, but it doesn't hurt to do the research since you're already interested in it anyway.

Before moving on, ask yourself these questions:

Does this feel like something that will be helpful on your journey?

If yes, in what specific way could you see this being helpful?

How does this fit (or not fit) into your GPS?

CONCLUSION

*"If you do right by people, work hard, and don't have kids
too early, you can have anything you want much easier."*

—MAMA SWEAT

A RICH, FULFILLING LIFE

My mother's life was hard as a child, and it was hard as an adult.
The difference is that she made it hard for herself as an adult. She
lacked the discipline to control her spending. She really liked
things, and if she wanted it, she'd get it, whether or not she could
afford it, which made her problems worse. If she had followed the
principles in this book, she could have had a rich, fulfilling life.

For the record, I like nice things too (I think my Lamborghini
proves that point nicely). However, I exercise more responsibility when buying my nice things. Because I make my purchases

the smart way, I make my life a little bit easier and less stressful while still getting nice things. However, I didn't really understand the impact of the cyclone of money until recently.

About a year ago, I saw how much my Lamborghini and Rolex appreciated, and it really hit me. Being able to take my love of cars and plug it into my cyclone of money really took me by surprise.

WHAT YOU (SHOULD HAVE) LEARNED

Congrats. You've made it to the end of the book. At this point, you should know what F-U Money is and what it means to you. You've learned what can get in the way of making it to F-U Money (having babies, popping bottles, living alone) and how to avoid them. You've learned how to set your GPS. You've learned about the four main vehicles to take on the path to F-U Money. And you've learned how to keep your money moving perpetually.

Now what?

The number one thing you need to do is take action. Don't fall into the trap of mental masturbation. What a lot of people do is learn how to make money but then sit on their ass and talk about it.

"I learned this about the stock market."

"In Tay's book, he talks about how to get into crypto."

Great, I'm glad you learned something. Are you utilizing any of your newfound knowledge?

HIRE A COACH

You have to use this stuff. Now that you know the secrets of the rich, follow them. If you feel like you don't have it together yet, or that you still need a little more guidance, hire a coach or get a mentor. A mentor is someone who, technically speaking, already has it figured out and is a few steps ahead of you, and they are willing to help you for free. If you can't find a mentor, then you need to find a coach. A coach is a mentor who charges you for access to their information.

What if you can't find a mentor and can't yet afford a coach? Then you need to read. Read as many books as you can. It may not be completely free—you may need to pay ten to twenty dollars—but compared to coaching and training, that's basically nothing. (However, definitely use your library as much as possible—just take notes on what you read so you can refer to it once you return the book.) Books are one of the best forms of mentorship. I used books as mentors when I first started out, especially *Rich Dad, Poor Dad* by Robert Kiyosaki. Kiyosaki was my mentor. Books are exactly what you get from mentors: information on how to do better, be better, and get to the next level. It's why authors (like me) write the book in the first place.

The big difference between a mentor and a coach is the level of dedication. Mentors give you something for free, so there's no motivation for them to show up. They can sometimes put forth a half-assed effort. Let's be honest: even if your mentor genuinely wants to help you, they won't be as in-depth and as great as they would if they were being paid to show up.

If you give a coach a lot of money to help you, their ass is going to be very motivated to help you. They are now obligated to help you. You gave them money, so they have to show up. They want to deliver you results because their name and their reputation is on the line. It goes both ways too. When you don't pay, you aren't going to take the lessons seriously. You're not going to do the work as well as if you paid, and therefore, your results won't be as good. There's even a saying about it: "The more you pay, the more you pay attention."

I've paid for coaches for every step of my journey, not just for finances and business but for my relationships too. I was a trainer and nutritionist for over ten years, and guess what! I still have a fucking trainer. I pay to have someone kick me in my ass when I'm not showing up and doing the work. If it's serious to me, I want a coach for it. I want someone who is going to be there and hold me accountable.

WHO HOLDS YOU ACCOUNTABLE?

You should also surround yourself with people who will hold you accountable. I have my health-nut friends and personal trainer to tell me when they see my body slipping. When I start getting out of shape, they'll tell me, "Hey buddy, have you looked in a mirror? Get it together." I have a financial guy who will tell me if I start spending too much money on frivolous things like new shirts. He'll tell me to stop and put that money into my stock or other assets.

If you don't have friends who can do this for you, buy them. Get yourself a personal trainer. Get yourself a financial coach. You don't need people who are just going to tell you how amazing you are all the time. That's not helpful. It may feel great being told how great you are doing (even when it's not true), but that's not going to get you ahead.

OPEN A BROKERAGE ACCOUNT

Even if you don't have a lot of money, open a brokerage account. Start working your way to a 70/30 split: 70 percent of what you make is for living, and 30 percent is for investment. "Hey Tay, I can't do a 70/30 split. I won't be able to live!" If you can't get to a 70/30 split right now, that doesn't mean you don't do the split. That means you adjust what you are spending money on so you can get your spending down to 70 percent and invest your 30 percent.

How? First, go back through the chapters. Do you need to move in with a roommate? Are you partying, smoking, drinking? Whatever you need to do to cut your expenses to put your 30 percent in your brokerage account, make it happen.

If you cut as much as possible and you are still struggling to do your 70/30 split, then you need to look for ways to increase what you make. Yeah, I'm talking about a side hustle or entrepreneurship.

If you're middle class and making $50,000, or $4,166 mothly *before* taxes. After taxes, that's about $2,000 a month, so if it's not enough for you to split, then start a side hustle to get an extra $500 so you're getting $2,500 a month. Thirty percent of $2,500 is $750 that you should put in your account every month, leaving you with $1,750 to live on.

TAKE CARE OF YOUR BODY

If you're not taking care of your body properly, it's going to affect your entire life. Fueling your financial performance starts with what you are putting into your body and how you're treating your body.

Drink water. Drink half your weight in ounces every day. If you weigh 150 pounds, you should drink seventy-five ounces of water every single day.

My goal has always been to outdo the competition. So, when my competition is eating breakfast, eating a snack, eating their lunch, washing all those dishes, taking a few shits (because healthy people have a fast digestive system), I'm working. I'm getting a leg up. I am out working.

WHAT'S NEXT?

I hope by reading this book you've learned how to be financially healthy and get rich. Unfortunately, a lot of people will not get this information based on their class ranking, skin color, or gender. I hope with this book I can break down these barriers and help you improve your life.

If this book helped you, keep an eye out for my next book. I plan to release a book a year in order to help people in all aspects of their lives. I've been through so much in my life that I have a lot of knowledge that can help other people. Books helped teach me throughout my journey, and now my books can help others.

ABOUT THE AUTHOR

Tay Sweat, author of *The Wild Rabbit,* is an entrepreneur and investor, known for his knowledge in fitness, health, business, and finance.

His journey began at age seventeen when he overcame clinical obesity, diabetes, and hypertension through self-education in fitness and nutrition. Working off 120 pounds showed him that he could accomplish anything, so he set his sights on escaping poverty.

Tay has since become an eight-figure millionaire through investments and multiple business ventures—all *without* going to college. Today, he continues to create wealth and now spends his time traveling, living out his dreams, and teaching others how to create F-U Money.

www.ingramcontent.com/pod-product-compliance
Lightning Source LLC
Chambersburg PA
CBHW031851200326
41597CB00012B/358

* 9 7 8 1 5 4 4 5 3 1 9 0 8 *